THE STRATEGY OF PERSUASION

ARTHUR E. MEYERHOFF

The Strategy of Persuasion

THE USE OF ADVERTISING SKILLS IN FIGHTING THE COLD WAR

INTRODUCTION BY EUGENE BURDICK

FOREWORD BY HARRY AND BONARO OVERSTREET

AFTERWORD BY

CONGRESSMAN DANTE B. FASCELL

Coward-McCann, Inc.
New York

Contents

INTRODUCTION

by Eugene Burdick

I DO not know if the answers which Mr. Meyerhoff gives in this remarkable book are true. If they *are* this is one of the most exciting books of our times. It may also be one of the most decisive. For Mr. Meyerhoff asks the proper questions. He asks the questions which have nagged, provoked and irritated Americans for the last two decades.

At the end of World War II it was difficult to believe that America's world position could possibly deteriorate. We alone possessed the atomic bomb. We alone had surplus food with which we fed both friend and former foe. We alone had the technical knowledge and the surplus capital with which the ravished industrial countries could be rebuilt. We alone had no history of colonialism. We alone had an unblemished prestige. We were, in honest fact, a sort of innocent colossus. We *knew* we were not imperialistic nor expansionist; we assumed everyone would know that also.

Almost twenty years later we look not merely innocent. We look maladroit and clumsy. Nor do we look so powerful. And, most surely, our prestige has faded badly. After spending over 100 billion on foreign aid, losing the lives of thousands of Americans and uncountable billions of private capital a strange thing has occurred: America is on the defensive.

Mr. Meyerhoff sketches in the proportions of this "decline" in a vivid manner. He then raises the question bluntly "Must the American decline be followed by a fall?"

Dozens of experts have addressed themselves to the question. Almost always their answers are cloudy, ambiguous, qualified and stress the many uncertainties of foreign policy. What is completely novel and striking about THE STRATEGY OF PERSUASION is that its answers are simple, dramatic and uncomplicated. They have the ring of truth about them.

This book is not elegantly written and this is deliberate. This book must offend a large number of people, for the author, with a refreshing casualness, names those whom he thinks have done a poor job. This also is deliberate. Mr. Meyerhoff has the presumption to tell political scientists what has been flawed with American foreign politics. And this, also, was deliberate. It is also overdue. As a political scientist I have long had the feeling that politics is too important to leave to either politicians or political scientists.

The central argument of this book is that the American colossus in its concern with vast armament and sweeping foreign aid programs never developed the fine sensitive fingers which allowed it to grapple with the most subtle and elusive part of politics: persuasion. What is maddening about the situation is that America has developed the arts of persuasion to the highest degree. Unfortunately the art is something known as "advertising" and, as every well informed college graduate knows, advertising may be able to sell corn flakes, but it cannot sell democracy. A tradition emerged that politics was the province of journalists or politicians or professors or bureaucrats, but it should not be sullied by the chill commercial hand of advertising. The advertising community might not agree, but tradition has a way of becoming very rigid, very soon. Mr. Meyerhoff is not a man with a high respect for tradition. For this he deserves our applause.

What he proposes is that American advertising skills and knowledge be made a strong arm of American "propaganda." He does not call it "public information" or any of the other sweeter names. He calls it "propaganda" and that is precisely what it is.

It is an argument which I have always found peculiarly unconvincing. I was one of those that did not believe you could "sell democracy the way you sell corn flakes." This book has caused me to revise my opinion. In short, with one non-believer, it has been persuasive. I have the lingering suspicion it will be persuasive with a good many others.

It deserves to be persuasive. In his own way Mr. Meyerhoff shows the kind of insight that Lenin showed when he invented the slogan "Peace, Land, Bread" and, by repetition and simplicity made a revolution almost single-handed.

This is, as far as I know, the most convincing argument I have seen that advertising, that peculiarly American institution, could be formed into a powerful weapon in foreign policy. This is a fascinating book to read, but not exactly pleasant. It is intriguing, but is never soothing. It is a hard book, but then we live in hard times. I commend the book to fellow Americans and hope that they will act on what they read.

Honolulu, Hawaii
August, 1964

By Harry and Bonaro Overstreet

THIS is a time when every citizen of conscience searches his mind for what he can best do for his country. That citizen thinks best who starts from what he knows best.

This book is the product of the skilled thinking of one such citizen. He has had back of him a lifetime of experience in the field of selling. His vocation has been selling. His avocation, however, has been that of putting every skill of the advertising profession at the disposal of good causes. In this book he asks that the skills of his profession be placed more fully than they have been at the service of the noblest of all causes—the defense of freedom.

We have the feeling that this book may well have in it a new breakthrough for our Cold War strategy. We, too, have something to sell—a great human idea and way of life. We have to sell it to bewildered peoples just emerging out of social and political infancy; we have to sell it to enslaved peoples behind various Iron Curtains in order to keep up their hope and courage; we have to try to sell it to those who have been lured into the pseudo-science of Marxism-Leninism, and who, in their ideological delusion, seek to take over the world; finally, we have to re-sell it to ourselves lest we grow listless in defense of a freedom we merely take for granted.

In short, in spite of our enormous and indispensable preoccupation with military strategy, we are fighting a psychological war: a war for the minds and hearts of men. This is the essence of what this book is about. And it is for this that it offers its services.

Selling Democracy Abroad

THE United States has not sold itself to the world,"
Lyndon B. Johnson said when, as Vice-President, he returned from a tour of foreign nations in 1961, appalled by
the ill will toward this country which he had found. "A
nation that knows how to popularize cornflakes and luxury
automobiles ought to be able to tell the world the simple
truth about what it is doing and why it is doing it."

On the basis of our skill in selling our products, we have
built the most prosperous democracy in history. Yet we
have not effectively applied our sales techniques to selling
ourselves and our ideas to other countries. We put billions
of dollars into military assistance, economic aid, and cultural programs in foreign countries; but our government
still has no organized and coordinated program for presenting our image to other peoples; and every attempt to
apply our advertising skills to propaganda has met with
official antagonism and public apathy.

And while we are failing to sell ourselves, our adversary,

the Soviet Union, is hard at work falsifying our ideals and intentions in the eyes of other countries, and promoting a distorted view of its own system.

"The Communist propaganda machine," Attorney General Robert F. Kennedy has written, "constantly spews forth its facts and figures and its version of how to solve the problems of the world. It broadcasts the line that the Soviet Union and Communist China hold the correct philosophy and that the United States is aways in error. . . . The U.S. . . . is to them a system of 'capitalistic imperialism,' and everyone from Marx to Khrushchev knows just how cruel and aggressive that system is. . . .

"No one comes forward with an explanation of the modern-day United States; no one counters with the fact that modern-day colonialism is tied to Communism, not capitalism. No one is there to talk about Latvia, Lithuania, Hungary, Poland, Tibet, or East Germany and East Berlin. No one is prepared to counter the Communists' arguments with facts and figures. . . ."

For decades the Communists have spent billions on research and experiment, training propagandists and agitators, and spreading a network of broadcasts, publications, and field agents over the entire world. They have created a propaganda machine which excels that of any other country on earth. Not even the United States seems able to marshal its forces to reach men's minds on such a scale.

The tragic irony is that the very means by which the Soviets have outstripped us were developed in the United States by the advertising industry. The techniques of persuasion by which the Russians seek to subvert governments, win the allegiance of new countries, and turn every political situation to their own advantage, are fundamentally the same psychological devices that we apply daily in selling products to consumers, and selling ideas at home.

One reason that the United States has not sold itself to the world is that the job has never been given to the people who know how to do it. These are the people who have popularized cornflakes and automobiles, and they are skilled in the art of persuasion, which is the basis of successful propaganda. We as a nation are wary of propaganda. Our distaste for it comes partly from the hastily improvised and often crude propaganda which we remember from the first World War, and from the unscrupulous uses to which the Russians have put it. It does not seem to us democratic; and we overlook the fact that two of the pioneers of our freedom and democracy, Thomas Paine and Thomas Jefferson, were also our first propagandists; and that the Declaration of Independence is as revolutionary a document as the Communist Manifesto. We are prejudiced against advertising as "hidden persuasion." When it is suggested that our skill in persuasion be applied to our propaganda effort, we hear the objection "You can't sell democracy like soap flakes," and the idea is dismissed.

Our reluctance to engage in an effective propaganda effort is proving advantageous to the Communists. Since 1917, their system has advanced steadily, with few major setbacks and none which they regard as permanent. While we congratulate ourselves on having achieved a lull in the Cold War in the West, the long-range Communist propaganda war goes on unabated. It is not merely a supple-

ment to the Soviets' military threats; it is part of their
ideological plan for world domination, and their efforts
never slacken. The Communists take advantage of the atmosphere of peace to win new concessions—treaties, trade
agreements, nuclear arms pacts, and cultural exchanges
become propaganda weapons for them.

Of course, like every other nation, we have always carried on propaganda activities of a sort. The United States
Information Agency, which has the responsibility of disseminating information about our country abroad, has
disputed Robert Kennedy's statement that there is no one
to counter Communist falsehoods about us: the USIA is
active in every country where there is an American Em-
bassy. But such observers as Lyndon Johnson, Robert
Kennedy and Richard M. Nixon have found little evidence
that the USIA effort has borne fruit.

The USIA is staffed by able, intelligent, and conscien-
tious men, but they are not trained in the art of persuasion.
As a result, the message which they bear does not reach
the people for whom it is intended in a form that has
meaning for them.

It is precisely here that men and women skilled in advertising techniques can be of use to the government. The
advertising industry is experienced in selling ideas as well
as products. The Advertising Council has contributed its
skills voluntarily to the government in such areas as public health, conservation, and Defense Bond campaigns.
Advertising men have long advocated the systematic ap-
plication of their skills to an institutional campaign on
behalf of the United States and the ideals of democracy.

Charles H. Brower, chairman and chief executive of

Batten, Barton, Durstine & Osborn, fourth largest advertising agency in the country, in suggesting that the government name a Secretary of World Affairs, with Cabinet rank and authority, in charge of U.S. "ideological warfare," has outlined some basic requirements for the task:

We need a sales manager. We need an advertising manager. And we need a staff in the field—and the field in this case is the whole world. And we either ought to get it, or ... we ought to stop wondering why our international sales curve continues to drop, month by month, and year by year.... I think there should be a department dedicated wholly to selling the United States to other nations—just as importantly—to itself....

For more than twenty years the Advertising Council ... has worked to help our country at home. Last year [1960] its members contributed $182 million worth of advertising to such causes as Defense Bond sales, the United Fund campaigns and Red Cross drives. It helped take the census, helped get out the vote. It worked to increase teachers' salaries, to increase school capacities— and a dozen other projects.

Here is proof that advertising can be used to sell ideas. Here are the men who have proved that they are willing to work for their country and that they can work effectively....

And I do not even suggest that the Advertising Council be used. I merely point out that our government needs help ... and that people trained in advertising can give that help....

We must realize that psychological war—call it cold war, if you will, or a war of nerves—wins victories just as important, just as historical and just as permanent as a shooting war.

Our effort in this field must cease being a part-time

job, or a short-change job ... for any good job of selling America would not just combat slander, not just clear our name, not just defend. It would give a pattern that other less privileged peoples could adapt to their own needs—a pattern of a dynamic, fluid, working democracy —economic as well as political.

The more people who understand America, the better chance for the survival in the world of everything America stands for. And who will understand America until the job of making America understood is put into the hands of people who know how to sell?

THE STRATEGY OF PERSUASION

⋆   **I**   ⋆

The Soviet Propaganda Offensive

SUPPOSE the West were to suddenly give in and grant all of Moscow's demands, would that lead to good will?" Maxim Litvinoff, a former Soviet diplomat, was asked this question more than a decade ago.

"It would lead to the West being faced, after a more or less short time, with the next series of demands," he replied.

Mr. Litvinoff, Ambassador to the United States from 1941 to 1943 and later Soviet Deputy Minister of Foreign Affairs, succinctly summed up the Communist strategy.

It is a strategy that the Soviets have employed with considerable success ever since they emerged as a world power bent on world domination after the last war. It is by no means the only device they have used, but it has become a familiar one to the nations of the West; and it illustrates the seriousness and the urgency of their intentions, the deadly purpose that lies behind all their political acts and the propaganda advantages which they gain from them.

For years we have watched a baffling series of political gambits and an increasing barrage of agitation and propaganda: the Communists have brought the eastern European nations that touch their borders into their system; they have made factitious political alliances, then repudiated them; they have smilingly welcomed negotiations with the West, then angrily refused them; they have tried to gain power in remote neutral nations; they have infiltrated the political movements of every country in the world; and all the time their propaganda machine has blanketed the entire globe with literature and broadcasts denouncing the "imperialists" and advocating Communism.

The whole world has been dragged into a political and ideological struggle that began when the Bolsheviks took over state power in Russia. The Western world has been reluctant to engage in this struggle; but since the end of World War II there has been no choice.

The present period has been defined as one of "Ideopolitics" by Kalijarvi and his associates in the book *Modern World Politics;* that is, one wherein states or cliques within states have made the manipulation and exploitation of the minds of men the basis for obtaining, enlarging or perpetuating political power.

Communist political devices, agitation and propaganda are not a new development; they have been an integral part of the Marxist-Leninist theory of revolution from the very start. Russia's steady march toward world domination is part of an overall plan in which the conquest of men's minds plays an indispensable role. Josef Stalin wrote in his *Foundation of Leninism:* "It is the essential task of the victorious revolution in one country to develop and support the revolution in others. So the revolution in a victorious country ought not to consider itself as a self-contained unit, but as an auxiliary and a means of hastening victory of the proletariat in other countries."

The aim of Communism is to win world power through influencing men's minds in the areas of social, economic and political values. We have been facing the menace of Communism since its beginnings more than forty years ago; today we face a greater threat than we faced last year, last month or last week.

The political power of the Communist movement began in 1917—it is not yet a half-century old. Yet since its precarious beginnings it has gained territory and converts faster than any other religious or political movement in the history of the world.

The Communists have not done this by cloaking the aims of their ideology in secrecy; there has been, from the very first, an overwhelming amount of information about Communism.

The story of Communism begins in Berlin in 1837. Karl Marx, a rebellious, brilliant student, joined a company of young philosophers (the *Doktor Klub*) who were disciples of Georg Wilhelm Friedrich Hegel.

Although Marx did not accept all of Hegel's philosophy, he saw in Hegel's theory of dialectics (a continuing evolution through thesis, antithesis and synthesis) a pattern of political struggle evolving from human progress.

In 1844 Friedrich Engels, the son of a well-to-do manufacturer, and crusader against the intolerable working conditions in factories of that era, joined forces with Marx in a partnership that lasted nearly forty years. Marx and Engels, in their *Communist Manifesto,* printed in 1848, outlined a new hard philosophy and guide to social action.

Marx applied Hegel's theory of dialectics to economics: The capitalists, or bourgeoisie, who exploited the working classes, were the "thesis"; those who were exploited (the workers) were the "antithesis"; and out of this struggle would grow a synthesis. For Marx, the synthesis "capitalism" was the outgrowth of a struggle that overthrew "feudalism." He believed that capitalism was now ready to be overthrown in a struggle that would result in a new synthesis—Communism.

Marx knew it would be difficult. In the *Communist Manifesto* he says:

> All previous historical movements were movements of minorities, or in the interest of minorities. The proletarian movement is the self-conscious, independent movement of the immense majority. The proletariat, the lowest stratum of our present society, cannot stir, cannot raise itself up, without the whole super-incumbent strata of official society being sprung into the air.... The proletariat of each country must, of course, first of all settle matters with its own bourgeoisie.

Marx looked on capital as a social, not a personal, power, and the only way he saw to destroy this social power was to divest the bourgeoisie of the ownership of the means of production.

He warned that the bourgeoisie would fight the changes he proposed. He directed these words to them:

> You are horrified at our intending to do away with private property. But in your existing society private property is already done away with for nine-tenths of the

population.... You reproach us, therefore, with intending to do away with a form of property, the necessary condition for whose existence is the non-existence of any property for the immense majority of society.... You reproach us with intending to do away with your property. Precisely so; that is just what we intend.

No dreamer, Marx realized that there was no easy method of taking power from the hands of the bourgeoisie. In another section of the *Communist Manifesto*, he said:

Of course, in the beginning this cannot be effected except by means of despotic inroads on the rights of property....

The philosophy of Marx and Engels found a ready advocate in the revolutionary socialist, Nikolai Lenin, who made his way back into Russia after the outbreak of the revolution in March of 1917, and, in November 1917, overthrew the Kerensky regime (Russia's one brief attempt at a democratic government), executed the Tsar and his family and established a "dictatorship of the proletariat."

Lenin was the first of the iron men of Communism; a violent fanatic, he was at the same time a political genius of the first rank and the most significant personality of his period.

Joseph Vissarionovich Stalin took up the mantle of power in Communist Russia following Lenin's death in 1924. He was a tremendous personality, a shrewd politician and student of Marxism.

Stalin ruled by a cult of personality and abysmal cruelty. Both Stalin and Lenin distrusted their own people; Marx held that the proletariat would rule the world, Lenin saw to it that his political core ruled the proletariat. Stalin expanded this power during a period of cruelty unsurpassed in modern history, and its autonomous rule gave the Communist Party a resiliency and a boldness that has enabled it to take advantage of its enemies—the free peoples of the world.

Nikita Sergeyevitch Khrushchev, who finally succeeded Stalin after a three-year power struggle (1953 to 1956), has given every indication of providing the Communist Party with even more flexibility by his seeming intention to end the "rule by personality."

This bodes no good for the free world. The basis of Communist politics remains the manipulation of people, whether they wish to be manipulated or not, with the simple political objective of *power*.

Under Khrushchev a new facet has been added to the techniques already in possession of the Communists. Khrushchev has developed the dimension of "unbalance"; by shrewd political propaganda he has alternately put the free world off balance, let it regain its equilibrium and then thrown it off balance again. He has used every dialectical tactic known to Communism to achieve this continual imbalance.

The Communist goal of absolute power is very simple. The methods used are devious, but they are not secret.

Long ago Lenin laid down the rule that wherever possible the Communist Party would be a "legal" power. But beside this legal power there always would be an illegal area of the Party which would remain hidden, even from the members who belonged to the legal Party. Like Lenin and Stalin, Khrushchev does not trust the people. Most members of the Communist Party are never told the current objective of the party or the methods by which these objectives will be obtained.

Lenin formulated this law and practiced it assiduously. He was a member of the Bolshevist Party, then a wing of the Socialist Party. He worked to bring down the Kerensky government in the November Revolution of 1917 by infiltrating the workers' council in Petrograd. Lenin also devised the tactic of infiltration through other public organizations.

Stalin doggedly carried out the infiltration concept in many countries with brilliant results.

The downfall of Czechoslovakia is a prime example of such infiltration. The coup was a peaceful one. President Beneš's coalition government, torn with dissention, hoped to bring peace to the Czechoslovakian people. In its tremendous desire for peace, the government gave office to several Communist leaders. Within a period of two years, from 1946 to 1948, the cadres of hardened Communists who had infiltrated scores of public organizations had put the government into a squeeze impossible to escape. Aided by the Communists in government posts, the hidden cores of Communists in public organizations (the Youth Federation, the Friends of the Soviet Union, the trade unions, etc.) agitated successfully against government policies, and the Social Democrats of Czechoslovakia were forced to the wall. The government dissolved, and the Communists took over.

The experiment in Czechoslovakia taught the Communists a valuable lesson: A country can be taken over without armed revolution *if the bourgeoisie can be induced to go along quietly.*

Nikita Khrushchev learned these lessons well at the knee of Josef Stalin. In addition he has learned the lessons of subtlety and patience. He strongly backs seemingly insignificant groups in foreign countries, inspires them to apparently harmless actions, then waits for a long-term gain. Inseparable from his ultimate goal is propaganda, for which he makes use of the free world's vast network of communications to give a false color to the image of Communism. Just as the Chinese Communists came to power as "agrarian reformers," and Castro was pictured as the liberator who would give Cuba true independence, so Khrushchev projects an image of himself as a worker in behalf of world peace.

He knows that if at the proper moments he comes out in favor of world peace, then bares the steel fist under the velvet glove by a display of military might, sincere non-communist peace groups in other countries will make appropriate demonstrations. It is one of the tasks of the hidden Communists in this country to align themselves with such groups for the primary goal of influencing our government. One example of the way in which Communists make political acts serve propaganda purposes can be found in the peace demonstrations that followed the Russians' explosion of their 50-megaton bomb. It was the Soviets' purpose to transfer the antagonistic feelings about this act to the United States or other free nations. With perfect timing, on November 1, 1961, two days after the bomb was set off, there was protest in the United States from large groups of women who went so far as to picket

our army headquarters. This was a predictable result of
the bomb explosions and the harsh talk that preceded
them. The Russians knew that a spontaneous uprising of
people who deeply desired peace above all else could be
motivated. And it was.

I am sure that none of the sincere mothers who pro-
tested en masse has any love for Russia, and that most of
those women are deeply devoted Americans who would
offer their sons for the defense of the United States. Nevertheless, Russia made every one of them a tool in this
never-ending battle of the Cold War. Their protests were
made to all nations, although the USSR was the only
country exploding nuclear weapons at the time. Telegrams
were sent to both Khrushchev and President Kennedy—
thus putting Kennedy in the same category as Khrushchev.

The peace demonstrations were of course duly reported
by newspaper and radio stations all over the world because they were in fact news; and thus Khrushchev made
the free press of the Western nations and others a chan-
nel for his propaganda.

The protest to Khrushchev would hardly reach the Russian people. However, the protest to Kennedy urging
peace was relayed to the Russian people, but the fact that
Khrushchev *was* included in the pleas was not divulged.
If the message had been aimed only at Khrushchev,
who was responsible for those nuclear tests, Russian propaganda would not have been served. When the protests
were aimed equally at our President and at the Soviet
leader, it left an onus of guilt on America in the minds
of many Americans and other peoples who did not realize
that President Kennedy was attempting to accomplish the

same purpose diplomatically that the well-meaning women tried to accomplish with peace marches.

Late in 1962 a Congressional Committee conducted an investigation of an organization called Women Strike for Peace. The Chicago *Daily News* in an editorial subsequently said:

> The opponents are trying to make it appear that the investigation is at best ungallant and at worst illegal. Apparently neither women nor the cause of peace should ever be suspect.... The sad fact is that the female of the species is not invariably a paragon of perfection and the cause of peace is sometimes used as a cover-up for sinister motives.
>
> No one, as far as we know, has charged that Women Strike for Peace was a Communist-inspired organization. The committee made it clear before hearing the organization's founder that there was no evidence she had ever been entangled in any way with the Communists.
>
> The same cannot be said for some of the subordinates in the group. Several women ducked behind the Fifth Amendment to avoid questions about prior Communist connections. Their failure to answer inevitably leaves the impression that however innocently it began, the women's peace group has attracted Communist attention, particularly in New York. If this proves to be the case, it won't be the first time.
>
> The Communists, unfortunately, have almost succeeded in slapping a copyright on "peace" by appropriating the term for their own groups and infiltrating Western organizations of sincere pacifists. They are past masters in the art of using people who are merely naïve as camouflage for subversion.
>
> Older organizations have had to learn this lesson or go down the trail toward disgrace and oblivion.... The

women who are genuinely intent on "striking for peace" had better take another look at the record of similar organizations and the need for vigilance in their own. . . .

Little more than a month after this editorial appeared, Lola Belle Holmes, who for six years worked as an undercover agent for the FBI reporting on Communist Party activities in the U.S., named Women Strike for Peace among the organizations that the Communist Party has attempted to influence or control.

Over the years, the Communists have become quite adept at using worthwhile causes to serve their own ends —either by infiltrating and misdirecting honest groups, or by setting up their own front organizations to direct popular support.

The creation of false images, the dissemination of misleading views on Russia's strength and intentions, are part of the Communist strategy. If Khrushchev can make the peoples of the free world believe that he is not unfriendly, he will have that much more scope for carrying out his plans.

It is easy to assume that two great nations, Russia and the United States, are locked in a struggle for world power that the advent of nuclear retaliation has neutralized. If the issue were this clear we would be well justified in relaxing our fears about Communism; it follows that since both the major powers in this struggle have the ability to destroy with retaliatory attack there will be no war. And, if we follow this line of reasoning, it is easy to imagine that Russia will be forced, at some time in the near future, to seek out alliances with free countries—even the United States—to meet the danger of a nuclear-armed China.

Some of our most knowledgeable columnists—Walter Lippmann for one—make this assumption. And logically, this assumption leads to the view that we are coming to an era in which we will have "spheres of influence," as in the nineteenth century, that will result in both great powers residing in peace, even though an uneasy peace.

This is precisely what Khrushchev wants us to believe. If this idea can be spread then the neutral nations today will be content—indeed, they will feel that they are wise— to remain neutral. Khrushchev wants them to remain neutral so long as he cannot take them over.

But Russia is not aiming at a nineteenth-century "sphere of influence" status. Khrushchev is dedicated to the eventual overthrow of every country in the world that does not now embrace Communism. He does not aim at a balance of power; he wants all of it. He does not strive for a "peace" of any dimension, his goal is the subjugation of the entire world.

Consider the immense barriers Khrushchev has surmounted since he came to power. When Stalin died he left a Party that was feared and hated throughout Russia. Khrushchev has sought popularity and has attained it without once relaxing his hold on the throttle of power. He has reformed (to a large degree) the rule of terror by the secret police. He has given writers and artists some freedom (though not much). He has tried hard to increase the flow of consumer goods to the people of Russia and he has succeeded to a degree. He has given the Soviet scientist a new status. Unlike his two powerful predecessors, he has traveled the world. Among the leaders and peoples of the uncommitted countries he has created an image that is not completely unfavorable.

He has emphasized, over and over again, that he has three objectives: Peaceful Coexistence, Anti-Colonialism and the Eventual Triumph of Communism.

Let us examine these three objectives briefly.

"Peaceful Coexistence" is a mouth-filling phrase. To the Western World it means that we will live in peace with Russia. To Khrushchev it means something quite different, and the meaning that Khrushchev takes is well understood by all Communists. It means, bluntly, the era between the emergence of Communism and the disappearance of capitalism. It means, to Khrushchev, that the machinery of infiltration must be stepped up, that the agitation for peace that can lead to conciliation must be increased. It means, in essence, the activation of every piece of Communist machinery to bring the uncommitted countries to the point of surrender to Communism. It does not mean living in peace with the world.

Anti-Colonialism does not mean, as it does to the free world, abolishing oppressive methods of government and the independence of colonial peoples. To the Communist, Anti-Colonialism is a pose based on Lenin's belief that stirring up the resentment of colonial peoples is the way to attack capitalism at its weakest point.

The Communist world seeks to isolate the newly emerging countries from all Western influence. This isolation has a twofold purpose: first, to prevent the emerging countries from contributing economically to the power of the West; second, to promote to places of power in the newly emerging countries persons who are sympathetic to the Communist cause. To this extent Khrushchev has supported such leaders as Nkrumah, Sukarno and many others. Russia's problem now is to keep these countries from falling into the camp of the West.

Indonesia is an example. The Communist Party in Indonesia (the PKI) now has approximately one million members and is a legal party. It supports Sukarno's official programs. It has long worked with the peasants and with those groups that seem to be traditionally dissatisfied—the schoolteachers and the college students. It has worked for land reform. It has infiltrated the cultural and religious societies. It even supports the belief that Allah is the One God!

In other countries freed from colonialism the Communist Party works in different ways. Economic aid is a prime mover in many cases. Since he does not have to compete with free industry in Russia, Khrushchev can pay exorbitant prices for the output of colonial countries. Khrushchev has already allocated some $5 billion in credits to secure trade with colonial countries. President Nasser of Egypt, for example, has now reached the point where his country is almost totally dependent on Russia for economic existence; Russia has purchased nearly the entire Egyptian cotton crop since 1956.

With economic aids, infiltration of cultural areas and official government bodies, and the studied isolation of newly emerging countries from the influences of the West, the Communists work religiously toward what they believe will be the eventual victory of Communism as a total world power.

Particularly effective have been the "wars of national

liberation" begun in weak nations. Allen Dulles, former head of the United States Central Intelligence Agency, said in April, 1964, that the U.S. does not have enough information about the strength of the subversive forces that operate in these countries. The Communist subversive effort, he said, "is not fully understood in the United States." He recommended that "the kind of study we applied to missiles, airplanes and other military problems" be applied to underground warfare also.

When Stalin died, Khrushchev faced the almost impossible job of bolstering morale in his country to carry forward the Communist ideology of eventual world domination. He has, in less than a decade, restored that morale and re-instituted belief in that goal. His scientists have accomplished tremendous feats in space technology and he has laid down one of the most ambitious programs of power that Russia has ever had. Khrushchev has promised his people that by 1970 there will be an abundance for all of his people; that hard labor will have vanished; that the use of money will have lessened to the point where it no longer will be a measure of affluence or comfort.

Khrushchev's speech containing his promises to the people of Russia ran to some 50,000 words. It is a feast of material for study by Western diplomats—indeed, by all free men, everywhere. In the speech Khrushchev does not set, as did his departed leaders, any definite time; there is no concrete "Five-Year Plan" or "Ten-Year Plan." Instead, Khrushchev has set the 1980's as the end of the period necessary to lay the full groundwork for the takeover of the world by Communism, and the eventual victory is postponed to some time in the future after 1980.

As do all good Communists, Khrushchev believes fanatically in the eventual victory of Communism, and this confidence that Communism *must* conquer the world in due time is a source of tremendous strength. The very fact that Khrushchev has set a date beyond his normal life-span underlines to the average Russian the inevitability of the Marxist concept of world rule.

This world struggle cannot be resolved into a stalemate with two great powers existing in peace because both are too strong to risk war. The war is on now and it has been, in one form or another, since 1917. There will be only one end to this war. Either the Communists will conquer the world or they will be forced into defeat by the mass education of the world against their ideology and the ultimate internal dissolution of the ideology among its own people.

Time works on the side of the Kremlin. The longer the free world delays meeting the challenge of Communism the better the war goes for the Russians.

It is time to meet the challenge by creating one of our own. Khrushchev depends in great measure upon the lassitude and the desire for peace of the free peoples; he will have to change his tactics if the free peoples of the world take a hand in this struggle and begin to change the course of history.

Supposing, as some people advocate, that all nuclear weapons would be outlawed, even by Russia. This would not change the course that Russia has set for itself. Military weapons are not the main issue in this conflict; the weapons threat is only one kind of propaganda ammunition.

Supposing we turn to pure negotiation, a stand advocated by many prominent thinkers in the world today. Where do we start?

Obviously, with dividing the world. That is what we have been doing since 1941 and in that time the Communists have gained more ground and enslaved more peoples than in any other period of world history. The Soviet strategy is based on piecemeal conquest and hot-and-cold propaganda gains. To negotiate the division of the globe would be only a fresh start for the Communists.

Should we fight, now? I say yes, but not with weapons and the lives of men. There is a clear indication Khrushchev has no intention of risking a nuclear war and that his threats are part of his propaganda program to take over the world peacefully. It appears that whenever the free world takes a positive stand he backs down.

Our best means of resolving this dilemma are purely political. We must change the course of history by changing the political climate of the free countries, the marginal countries and those countries now emerging into independence *through a program of persuasion.* People not yet in the Communist fold must be thoroughly indoctrinated in the dangers of Communism and the benefits of freedom.

The Communist Manifesto, the teachings of Marx and Engels, provides no guidance in the event the Communist march to world domination is halted. They assumed, from the first, that human nature could be changed to their way of thinking. There is no blueprint for action if their plan to alter human nature is stopped.

Communism is not all-encompassing, it is not all-powerful, it is not all-knowing. No Communist country has ever succeeded in creating or maintaining an agricultural society capable of feeding that country. There are wide rifts within the Communist company of nations. Red China is a constant menace to Khrushchev; Tito is a thorn in his ideological side; his great grain baskets are not full. There are scores of weak spots.

We must, if we are to survive the threat of Communism, begin to take the initiative and bring the war of propaganda to the enemy's ground.

If we do not—we are lost. It is as simple as that.

II

How They Fight

RUSSIA is starving her own people to feed propaganda
to the world . . . it seems the whole idea of Communism,
or whatever they want to call it, is based on propaganda
and blood," Will Rogers, American humorist, newspaper
columnist and author, observed after a trip to Russia in
1928. "The Soviet government, it may be wrong, but no
one is going to stand up on a soap box either publicly or
privately and announce the fact about it. Over there your
criticism is your epitaph.

"You can ask a Russian any question in the world, and
if you give him long enough, he will explain their angle
and it will sound plausible. Communism to me is one-third
practice and two-thirds explanation."

Propaganda of the kind Will Rogers referred to is repugnant to most Americans; but even though we are
repelled by what *Printers' Ink* has aptly called "black
propaganda—lies, incitements to violence, suppression of
information, agitation, surreptitious support of pressure

groups," we should not overlook its uses nor dismiss it
without understanding how the Communists have made
it an instrument against which we must forge weapons of
our own.

The Soviets propagandized their own people first, of
course. From the very inception of the Communist movement, propaganda has been basic to the revolutionary
doctrines, a tool for influencing public opinion and creating a political climate favorable to Communist aims. From
the start Lenin emphasized the importance of knowing
the enemy. In his "Letter to a Comrade on Our Organiza-
tional Tasks," he said:

> Today we are faced with the comparatively simple task
> of supporting students demonstrating in the streets of a
> large town; tomorrow, perhaps, we may be supporting a
> movement of the unemployed. The day after tomorrow,
> perhaps, we may have to take a revolutionary part in
> some peasant revolt....
> The hard-core revolutionary must have a clear picture
> in his mind of the economic nature and the social and
> political features of the landlord, of the priest, of the high
> official and the peasant, their strong and weak sides; he
> must know all the catchwords and sophisms by which
> each class and each stratum camouflages its selfish striv-
> ings ... he must understand what interests certain insti-
> tutions and what certain laws reflect and how they reflect
> them.

In the early days, throughout Lenin's tenure and well
into the first half of Stalin's regime, the propaganda line
was openly revolutionary. The favorite slogan was *Workers of the world, unite!* Soon the Communists developed

an apparatus by which they blanketed their whole nation with anti-capitalist slogans.

Today, according to Marvin L. Kalb, former CBS correspondent in Moscow:

> Agitprop, Kremlinese for the Department of Agitation and Propaganda of the Communist Party, is a well-heeled, highly interlaced operation, using all the media of communication and every social, economic and educational institution, as well as the established framework of the Communist Party, to inform the people of the latest emphasis in the Kremlin line. It is an operation that has always been as cherished by the Soviet state as it has been inescapable by the Russian people.
>
> The key men in the operation are thousands of agitators and propagandists, who work through 315,000 "primary units," i.e., the factories, the farms, the schools, the offices. Their job is a basic one; to translate the esoteric language of ideological debate into the simplest possible terms for the 215,000,000 inhabitants of the Soviet Union. Ever since the publication of the *Manifesto* they have been engaged in a nationwide, face-to-face campaign, selling the basic propaganda points.

Agitprop, Kalb says, repeats the theme: *Only the imperialists led by the United States want war. The imperialists cannot be trusted—they are still aggressive, colonialistic, expansionist.*

And, of course, the old saw: *The Soviet Union stands for peace.*

Note that agitation and propaganda are carried on by the same department. Agitation, or direct action, is used to create situations in which spoken and written propaganda will be effective. The Soviets do not rely on the press alone.

The Russians have never made the mistake of thinking that propaganda should be used to promote only good feelings about its own system; they know that propaganda, to be effective, should condition public opinion and influence political reactions both favorable to Communism and against its adversaries.

That Communist ideas on propaganda have faithfully followed the basic pattern laid down by Marx and Lenin is shown in an article in *Pravda* for September 14, 1960:

> The whole point of propaganda lies in its effectiveness. The main task of Party Propaganda is to expound the ideas of Marxism-Leninism profoundly and comprehensively, to show their successful translation into reality in the course of the Party's struggle for the victory of socialism and Communism in our country, to teach how the theoretical riches accumulated by the Party are to be used in practical activity and developed creatively, and to rouse the working people in the struggle to translate the Party's policy into action and to rear active and stalwart fighters for Communism.
>
> The duty of Party propaganda is to reveal through vivid examples the advantages of the social order and of the Marxist-Leninist ideology and to summon the masses forward and inspire, mobilize and organize them for accomplishing the grand program for the construction of Communism in our country. Each Party organization must determine specifically which groups of the population still remain outside the range of ideological and political influence, what measures must be carried out and how many additional propagandists and agitators should be brought in so that every person may be reached.

The study of Marxist-Leninist theory has been organized in close association with the nature of the activity of various groups of the intelligentsia. Ideological tempering furthers the intelligentsia's creative and socio-political growth and helps it to strengthen its ties with production.

What is needed today is to avoid the cut-and-dried, to organize propaganda and agitation creatively and to search persistently for the keys to the heart and mind of every Soviet person.

To achieve what Lenin proposed, and what the Soviets still practice, it was necessary to shut off completely the free flow of information and to control the press absolutely.

The success that Russia had with propaganda in her own country, and later in her satellites, has led to massive efforts to export their ideas to the free world. Her campaign of open revolution reached its peak in intensity and fury during the Depression years in the United States. All of Communism's advocates in that era happily forecast that capitalism could never survive the rigors of the economic setback that for a time nearly paralyzed America.

But we survived despite one of the biggest Communist propaganda assaults ever waged up to that time. Books advocating the overthrow of the United States Government were printed and widely circulated. The Communist press here was very active; a ten-cent edition of Josef Stalin's *Foundations of Leninism* was widely circulated. According to Harry and Bonaro Overstreet, authorities on the Communist Party in the United States, the ten-cent book was the best possible selection for the Party's purposes in a depression era in America. "Rarely have the precise Leninist procedures for exploiting the problems, angers and miseries of human beings been more explicitly stated," say the Overstreets.

With the failure of propaganda aimed at provoking outright revolution, the Communists in 1935 changed their line, but not their ultimate goal. The tremendous outflow of propaganda suddenly became softer and no longer preached overthrow and revolution. The new line was built around new slogans. "Peace," for example, was the central core of much of the new propaganda. The Russians launched a mighty offensive against Fascism.

It was the failure of the Communists to inspire open revolution in Depression America that made necessary a reevaluation and revision of their tactics. Today, Communist agents are no longer identified with revolutionary movements, but they attempt to infiltrate any group that espouses a cause which could be triggered into action at the right time to serve their purposes. We have seen how they have made use of peace groups in America. Other targets include dissatisfied minorities, labor organizations, students, young intellectuals—anyone discontented with the status quo and agitating for change in the present policy.

Communist agents who insinuate themselves into such groups are not looking for revolution now; they are preparing the groundwork for the future "revolution" which, according to Communist doctrine, is inevitable. For the present, the discontent that results from agitation serves the Communist purpose. Communist agents will agitate for racial equality one day if it serves their aims, and will march against a sit-in demonstration another day if that will help their cause. Today's Communist "revolutionary" exploits any kind of unrest to stir up trouble, generate unpleasant publicity, and make the United States —or any free nation—look bad. But this type of "revolutionary" is cagey; since he can no longer publicly preach the Party doctrine, openly "advocating the overthrow of the American Government," he (or she) becomes aligned with a cause that is strongly and sincerely believed in by its followers. Such a person is difficult to detect among a group of marchers carrying banners espousing their cause.

Significantly, the abandonment of the line of violence by Soviet strategists ushered in a new concept in Russian strategy; they began to prepare propaganda with specific areas, specific countries, and special groups in mind. Propaganda became an aimed missile instead of a general "shotgun" proclamation of uprising and war.

The Overstreets, in their book *The War Called Peace,* note that Lenin first saw the need for unified propaganda in 1901 when he advocated an all-Russian political newspaper to bring local groups under leadership of the hard-core leaders of dissent. Lenin thought that without an all-Russian paper the local leaders and the total population would remain divided and incapable of unified action toward a common goal. The Nihilists in the Bolshevist organization resisted him strongly. To them any political action short of murder and terror was "armchair work."

Once Lenin came to power in 1917 he put into operation his plans for propaganda via an all-Russian newspaper. His plan still is in effect today in Russia. The strictly controlled Russian press serves two main functions —it prints what the Russian leaders want their people to know, and it prevents other ideas from taking root in Russian minds.

Khrushchev's modernized propaganda machinery has been permitting interviews and stories to appear occasionally in the Russian press that tell the free world's story to the Russian people. But this is only a device to convince the Russian people and others that there is no Iron Curtain. Immediately after these stories appear, they are attacked on a day-in and day-out basis, which neutralizes their effectiveness with the Russian people.

To control men's minds it is not enough to control a mere newspaper. Everything written and available inside Russia had to be either destroyed or rewritten to conform with the Leninist doctrine. Thus occurred the rewriting of history that most Westerners find so laughable. It was not vanity that prompted Lenin and Stalin to rewrite history books; it was the sheer necessity of making sure that no Soviet citizen would believe anything outside the Party line.

With the successful beginning of this maneuver inside Russia, Lenin turned to the outside world and set up a network of distribution for pro-Communist literature. As we have noted, the main theme of this first major outside propaganda assault was riot, revolution and the overthrow of existing governments. But in 1935, stung badly by the failure of this type of propaganda tactic in the United States (where conditions for the overthrow of capitalism seemed to them hopeful), the Communists turned to a more subtle type of propaganda. The Communists began tailoring propaganda especially for the countries and the ethnic groups within the countries they wanted to influence.

To keep the various international propaganda organizations in line with the central policy of the Communist Party there has been one chief source of policy. The Overstreets identify this source as follows:

> Just as the old "trade union press" had been designed, in Tsarist Russia, to serve the needs and orient the minds of local revolutionary groups, so the newspapers and magazines issued by each member party of the Comintern served both to channel to national audiences the international Communist viewpoint and to stimulate "correct" words and actions on the local and national scene. The pamphleteers went to work, also. Publishing houses were established to turn out books by Communists native to each country and to reprint Soviet books. And everywhere the mimeographing machines rolled out leaflets, teaching manuals, guides for speakers, petitions for mass circulation and one "excellent handbook for agitators" after another. So far as the Communist press is concerned, nothing has changed since the time of Lenin. . . .
>
> The Party has never abandoned the concept of having one publication to unify and direct the whole movement. . . . This, today, is the *World Marxist Review*. By mid-1959, it was being issued in Russian, Chinese, Dutch, French, English, Spanish, German, Italian, Swedish, Czech, Polish, Rumanian, Bulgarian, Hungarian, Japanese, Mongolian, Korean, Albanian and Vietnamese.[*]

In this one magazine the Party line is laid down on all subjects. If the Negro question in America is raised, the *World Marxist Review* has printed, or will print upon

[*] From *The War Called Peace, Khrushchev's Communism,* by Harry and Bonaro Overstreet. Copyright © 1961 by W. W. Norton & Company, Inc., New York, N. Y. By permission of the publisher.

request, the exact Party line. If an emerging country in Africa is in difficulty with the United Nations—or with the United States—the correct Party line is immediately forthcoming for guidance.

The entire Soviet publishing venture is a huge operation. It is estimated that in 1960 some 40,000,000 books and booklets were printed by the Soviets in the languages of countries not a part of the Soviet ring. Red China is reported to have printed some 10,000,000 such books.

The combined Communist countries print and distribute within the free countries of the world some 120 different magazines in more than 400 different languages.

On a recent trip through Mexico, I browsed at an open bookstore on a main street in Mexico City—one of many. Not only were there hundreds of books and magazines in Spanish conveying all the arguments of Soviet and Chinese Communists—but I was even able to buy "newspapers" whose stories had a Soviet slant, five expensively printed magazines full of solid Red propaganda, and a large book by Nikita Khrushchev, all in English!

The prices of these publication were of interest to me. A book that would sell in the United States for at least six dollars sold for 80 cents in Mexico. High-quality magazines, costly to produce, sold for pennies. The deficit, of course, is made up by the Communists.

The canny Communists overlooked no major language group. Publications in German, Russian and French also were displayed on the racks.

High-level leaders in Mexican political, economic, social and labor circles generally read English as well as Spanish. It's reasonable to assume the potent Red propaganda I saw finds its way into their hands. And, of course, the many, many books and magazines in Spanish at low prices make it easy for them to find their way into the Mexican people's hands.

What can these same readers find to counter all this anti-American propaganda?

Two American magazines are distributed throughout Mexico—in Spanish. Since both are put out for profit, the cost of just one approaches the price of Khrushchev's 783-page hard-cover book. In contrast to Red periodicals, neither of these is a government publication. They often criticize American government policies and people in a typical free-swinging American way.

This is fine at home—but hardly the sole answer to Communist propaganda abroad.

The barrage of Communist propaganda takes on tremendous force in a country that is beginning to emerge from the darkness of illiteracy. As India began to educate its great masses some years ago, the Communist press concentrated on that country. The first written propaganda to reach India from the Communist printing presses was carefully scaled to the new reading ability of the masses and the circulation was relatively small. Today India is the target for more than 4,000,000 books and almost 200 magazines annually from Communist countries. And chief among these are the children's books—usually distributed free of charge—that do not carry the Soviet line. What they do carry is a subtle message that Soviet books are "good," they are "fun," and they are desirable. The Communist message can come a little later—after the child has been educated to the idea that Soviet books are good to read.

No military campaign has ever been waged with more forethought, more preparation, or more unswerving dedication than the Soviet campaign of propaganda. Every country not now in the Soviet bloc is a target and the war is carried on relentlessly.

The Overstreets cite two approaches the Communists use to the general target: First, they try to reach numbers, regardless of type. This involves slogans, mass meetings, and petitions. Second, they subdivide the population into types and fit the appeal to the interests of each. (This, incidentally, is essentially what the advertising profession does when it researches the market to find out those interests to which the particular product will appeal.)

People in newly emerging countries must be convinced that their national independence is in no way threatened by their accepting Soviet aid and guidance. Persons in the West must be persuaded to see hope in the Communist brand of "peaceful co-existence" and to help build public opinion in its behalf. They need not like Communism or want it spread further. It is enough if their desire for the lessening of world tensions makes their judgments on Communism chiefly projections of their own Western value systems, so that the ominous "permanent revolution," so basic in Communist dogma, has no reality for them.

From U. S. Government reports on Communist propaganda activities in various parts of the world we know that the Communists continue to exploit themes developed for and tailored to a certain country and its problems.

For example, in Greece in 1960 the outlawed Greek Communist Party continually told the Greeks that the Communists were struggling for "peace, bread and democracy." The government report stated that although two of these slogans, "bread" and "democracy," referred ostensibly to matters of purely local concern, the "Communists always managed to tie them in with anti-West themes." And in Israel from January 1960 to June 1961 the most common Soviet message "continues to be the threat to the area from 'imperialism' in all its aspects." The report also stated the "specific criticism of U. S. 'imperialism' included a variety of indictments encompassing the entire scope of U. S. operations in the Middle East plus several fanciful allegations."

And similar reports for Latin America, Africa, South Asia, the Far East and other Middle Eastern countries tell the same story—propaganda tailored to the area, with constant repetition of phrases and ideas implanted and fostered over a period of time.

In carrying out their propaganda program, the Communists make wide use of two important media—people and the press. It is estimated that Russia alone trains 100,000 men and women each year to be propagandists or agitators.

One of the effective devices used by the Communists is the cartoon. Red cartoons are distributed widely for use in the press of neutral and uncommitted countries as well as behind the Iron Curtain. These cartoons tell a simple message over and over. Unlike the innocuous cartoons we distribute abroad, the Red cartoons are deadly serious. The United States, its President, its officials, its policies—

and often its staunchest allies—are portrayed always by symbols of evil. The pictures say we are monsters, without exception.

In these cartoons our offers of help to other lands are interpreted as being made solely to lure a victim into a cruel trap. Our workers are always shown as crushed slaves. Our politicians seek only to enslave anyone unwary enough to trust America for a moment.

These cartoons are crude and offensive, but vivid. The message is unmistakable. Here are some examples:

The Communists have been successful in their attempts to sell propaganda to the West. Allen Dulles, in an interview on *Meet the Press* in January 1963, warned that many ideas expressed first in Russian propaganda later are reprinted as facts in some of our own publications.

Nearly every Russian scientific paper or cultural activity had its inevitable Russian Communist propaganda hidden in it in some way. For example, a scientific paper sent to Northwestern University in the field of agriculture includes the following statements:

> We know that capitalistic production relationships retard the realization of scientific methods of transforming nature for the purpose of stimulating the productive forces and developing agriculture. The new production relationships in Socialist countries on the contrary, contribute to the efficient utilization of natural resources for the stimulation of agriculture.
>
> In the total volume of scientific and practical scientific research now being done in the field of geomorphology, in the number of specialists engaged in this research and in the breadth of range of theoretical questions of geomorphology and its application in practice, the Soviet

Union at present unquestionably occupies first place in the world.

Radio Moscow program guides which are mailed to thousands in the United States invite people to hear the "thoughts and aspirations of the Soviet people on world events." Every amateur Russian radio operator sends government-printed cards of acknowledgment to other people of the world with whom he communicates, and these carry propaganda statements.

The so-called "cultural exchange programs" between Russia and the United States are used as platforms for propaganda. Many Russians who come to the United States under the guise of cultural exchange have been groomed to downgrade our way of life and paint glowing pictures of theirs. As Frederick C. Barghoorn says in his book, *The Soviet Cultural Offensive:*

> Soviet citizens are expected, in all of their dealings with foreigners, to act as mouthpieces of official policy . . . [the mission of Soviet cultural diplomacy] is not merely the positive one of protecting the aspects of Soviet reality selected by the Soviet authorities for domestic and foreign disclosure and glorification. It has, in addition, a negative mission of considerable significance, which consists in vituperative criticism of aspects of foreign cultures deemed to be incompatible with Soviet values, as well as censorship, distortion, or denial of positive aspects of bourgeois cultures which, according to officially determined Soviet definitions of capitalism, are not supposed to exist. Soviet visitors to foreign countries are expected to do their part in preserving the official mythology.

Ironically, Professor Barghoorn was arrested on a trumped-up spy charge while visiting Russia in 1963. It is believed that his arrest was due in part to statements such as these and others, and that his release came only after strong intervention by the late President Kennedy.

Our concept of free speech justifies this type of comment by visitors to our country. But the American way of life also embodies the idea of "fair play"—if visiting Russians are allowed to use our public media to voice propaganda about their system and blatantly criticize our way of life, then Americans visiting Russia in similar capacities should theoretically be allowed to do the same. Of course, it doesn't work that way; the continuation of the Soviet system depends on isolation, half-truths and padded facts. In the USSR, most interviews with public figures from the United States are taped and only those parts which are thought to be harmless or useful to Russian propaganda are played back later.

A professor attached to the cultural exchange programs who has been to Russia on several occasions told me that the Russian government sends to America only those people who are trained and coached in propaganda techniques, ardent defenders of the Soviet system. On the other hand, Americans sent to Russia on similar missions carry out their cultural duties only.

The third in a series of American-Soviet Exchange Agreements signed in March 1962 provides for a wide variety of exchanges of persons whose talents range from meteorology and immunology to music and basketball. According to the Soviet and Eastern European Exchanges staff of our State Department, in 1962 there were about 340 groups of Americans touring the Soviet Union under this program, with an estimated 1,500 persons involved from the U.S. An equal number came here from the Soviet Union.

Americans who go behind the Iron Curtain in organized groups are normally exposed to an orientation lecture which seeks to prepare them for the strange world they will be entering. But there is nothing about the selection process or the orientation itself which assures that these semi-official ambassadors will be particularly well equipped to speak out for America. The briefing is conducted by informed U. S. government officials, who outline the kinds of problems they will meet. The only prepared material distributed by the U. S. Government is a single sheet which deals with such travel problems as passport controls, currency, etc.

Our government makes no effort to supply the answers Americans should give when controversial subjects arise. Travelers are advised to be well informed about the problems of the day and to be prepared to give factual answers to questions. Even on such issues as the race problem, the government's only comment is that the traveler should be factual in discussing the issue as he sees it.

Several non-profit organizations, working with the encouragement of the government, have produced some useful materials which are available to members of these exchange groups and to individual tourists who want them.

The organizations urge Americans to take advantage of any opportunity to say what they believe. Many of them, when they reach the Soviet Union, are interviewed by Soviet reporters or broadcasters. This can be very dangerous, briefing officers warn, since what Americans say will be taken out of its context or edited for Soviet propaganda use. American travelers are generally cautioned that their chance to speak out as Soviet visitors do here will be very limited.

Communist propaganda has undergone many changes of line and tactics since the Communist Party's early days. It has expanded, new techniques have been developed, and it has attained a skill, refinement and subtlety that make it increasingly dangerous.

It is reliably reported that the Soviet Ministry of Agitation and Propaganda now operates over 6,000 schools and has more than 375,000 agents in the field. It does not rely merely on the conventional means of propaganda—the press, radio, direct agitation in foreign countries, and the infiltration of organizations; it also uses psychological weapons with great success. It makes propaganda out of its own political acts, and it creates fake incidents in order to play upon universal fears.

We have seen how Khrushchev made the United States seem to bear the burden of guilt when he exploded the 50-megaton bomb. That is only one example of the way in which the Communists skillfully use world tensions. But in this and in other cases we can recognize elements of "selling" techniques, the same ones that are used in advertising to get people to buy a product.

Communism is sometimes thought to be a failure because the countries which live under its system have lagged behind the rest of the world economically. But the goal of Communism is not a bountiful life—it is world domination; and the Communists continue to expand their power throughout the world. They succeed in this partly because they employ techniques of salesmanship.

A salesman knows that his objective is to sell a product, not win an argument, and that his aim is best accomplished in a harmonious atmosphere. So he sets about establishing it.

"When opposition is intense," says Jesse S. Nirenberg in his book *Getting Through to People,* "indicating a conflict with the other person, it is pointless for you to apply your counter argument with equal or greater vehemence, since it only forces the other person to maintain a strong stand so as to keep the conflict unresolved. . . . At this point you should abandon your pressure. This will cause the other person to abandon his."

The Russians are trying to sell Communism, and they know that the best atmosphere for "making a sale" is the harmonious feeling that prevails after a period of tension has subsided, when a relaxed feeling pervades the air. In the past decade we have seen them presenting the same spectacle over and over. The Communists deliberately create tension, then make a "concession"; then they take advantage of the harmonious atmosphere that exists when a clash has been avoided.

They may produce this tension by halting or harassing an American truck convoy in East Germany. They may arrest an American in Russia on trumped-up spy charges. When the conflict is resolved—when pressure is withdrawn —relaxation sets in, the world breathes a sigh of relief, and people think, "Maybe we can get along with the Russians after all." In this pleasant climate, the Communists press for a further advantage. People do not feel inclined to examine what has really happened. In short, a fake incident has produced an artificial tension, which was then reduced by a phony compromise.

The Russians also make use of a simple advertising device which is called "pleasant feelings from association with pleasant things." Advertisers use it often—a pretty girl holding a cigarette, a baby fondling a bar of soap, beautiful lakes surrounding a can of beer.

When we see a Russian ballet troupe, hear a fine pianist, listen to the works of an eminent composer, we do not believe that such cultivated, gifted people could be the product of a system that is based on the non-dignity of the human individual. We are inclined to believe that they are the product of a highly civilized society. The Russians know that their ballerinas and musicians produce a pleasant feeling in American spectators and divert attention from political issues.

A trained advertising man or an experienced salesman could, if he studied Communist techniques, spot some of the basics of selling in Soviet strategy. One of them is to create a fear where none existed, or to play upon a real fear. It was the principle device used by the old-time medicine man in selling his wares. It seems outlandish to compare Khrushchev with a peddler of worthless medicine, but that is sometimes the role he plays, and he seems to sell a lot of snake oil.

The medicine man's technique was to warn of "sudden death from a simple cold," or "the terrible agony of overheated blood," and then sell his remedy to terrified listeners.

The Bomb—nuclear warfare—has become the center of

world fear; it could unquestionably bring about the worst chaos the world has ever known. Khrushchev has created the false impression that the Soviet government might unleash its atomic arsenal almost capriciously if it doesn't get its own way.

A study of speeches and remarks by Russian leaders would not bear out the fact that Russia is rocket-rattling; they talk mostly of peace and coexistence and disarmament. But they don't *act* that way. They create "incidents" in Berlin, they foment disorder in young nations, they behave very much like erratic and unpredictable hoodlums. And subtly, deliberately, they implant the idea in Western minds that "you better watch those Russians; they might push the button if they get mad enough."

The Soviets used this scare device, coupled with the more modern technique of subconscious motivation, to gain an important foothold in the Western Hemisphere—in Cuba. Russia's true objective, I think, was to establish a base there for subversion and propaganda throughout the Americas. The Kremlin knew the U.S. would not permit a foreign power to send large amounts of men and matériel to bolster the Castro regime at that time.

So Russia proceeded to send not only men and matériel, but missiles and other offensive weapons as well. When the U.S. discovered missiles in Cuba—as I believe Russia fully knew and intended it would—our government of course demanded their immediate removal.

This confrontation, in late 1962, created one of the most tense moments for the world since the end of World War II. Yet I do not believe that we were any closer to nuclear conflict at that point than at any time since 1945. Russia merely let events reach a peak of excitement, let every living soul meditate for a moment on the possibility of a nuclear holocaust.

Then in stepped the "peace-loving" Khrushchev, who announced that he would remove the missiles, and the world breathed easier. The "crisis" was over. So great was the letdown that the U.S. did not "press its luck" by further demanding the withdrawal of Russian men and equipment. As a result, Russia achieved what it set out to do in the first place—establish a propaganda base in this hemisphere without interference from the United States. She trotted out the missiles the same way the patent medicine advertisers used to display grim pictures of afflicted persons. The whole idea was to instill fear—a fear which only the medicine could conquer. (The importance of Cuba as a Communist base today was emphasized by Dr. Milton Eisenhower, expert on Latin-American affairs. Speaking on the television program *Meet the Press,* April 5, 1964, Dr. Eisenhower noted: "Through Cuba there is being spent in Latin America more than $100 million through Castro Communist cells penetrating student groups, labor groups, and causing trouble wherever they can and above all misrepresenting the United States and better elements of their country.")

This Russian technique is described in more scholarly fashion in a valuable book, *Protracted Conflict,* written by a team of four men who studied Communist strategy for the Institute of Foreign Affairs:

> While the Communists are reluctant to go to war, they do not hesitate to *threaten* war in order to scotch Western initiative. The use of war threats has assumed, since

the Soviet Union obtained nuclear weapons and missiles, added importance in Communist conflict strategy. Given the "balance of terror," the Communists, acting through proxies, can present the West with strategic *faits accomplis* and then invoke the specter of general war in order to prevent the West from taking forceful action in the defense of legitimate interests. At the same time, the Soviets' display of defiance in the face of Western power serves to convince the weaker nations that the Soviet Union stands ever ready to protect them against the encroachments of "neo-imperialism."

There is another aspect to this psychological game of "bombophobia" which Russia is playing, and that is this: Khrushchev realizes that most Western officials are responsible to an electorate, and that government leaders must remain popular to stay in office. He knows that if he manufactures a crisis, then backs down on the most dramatic point, the Western leaders are apt to accept this headline-making "victory," and not bring up the fact that Russia has, in the bargain, gained its real objective.

The role of propaganda in the entire Soviet scheme for world-domination is well documented in an article by Robert Finley Delaney in the United States Naval Institute proceedings. Mr. Delaney, who has held Foreign Service posts in Rome, Budapest and Vienna, and who is an expert in unconventional warfare for the U. S. Navy, writes:

> The United States, as the leader of a loosely knit alliance of free nations, faces a powerful doctrinaire adversary in the U.S.S.R. and its system of satellite allies linked internationally through a highly efficient conspiratorial network of Communist parties. The object of the struggle

is the world. It remains as Lenin predicted so long ago: "There is a world to be won," for which he demanded men, dedicated to the ideal of Communism, who would devote "the whole of their lives" to achieving the ascendancy of this essentially anti-human form of totalitarianism.

To achieve this goal the Soviets have carefully, skillfully, and ingeniously perfected a weapons system of conquest and infiltration which, until relatively recently in our own awakening, remained obscure and often mysterious. This concept of Soviet total war, "protracted conflict" as Professor Strausz-Hupé has so precisely put it, enabled Russian planners to integrate elements of conventional armed might with a startling array of unconventional tactical tools such as guerrilla movements, espionage, world-wide campaigns of propaganda and subversion, and an effective collection of political and economic warfare techniques.

III

Motivation and Manipulation

THE American press in recent years has taken note of the fact that advertising, once spurned as a capitalistic device, is now being more widely used in the Soviet Union. However, this is a far throw from advertising as we know it in the United States. In Russia there is only one source of goods, and the only brands are state-produced. The problem is to get the people to buy up the surplus that has resulted from overproduction.

The Russian concept of advertising—no competition, no real free choice, no chance for profit—is consistent with the Communist doctrine of manipulation. Although they haven't adopted the Western rationale behind advertising, the Soviets have adapted the American type of consumer advertising to their own rationale. And for their world propaganda program, they have been drawing for some time on the same techniques as advertising uses.

Ironically, advertising men in America have gained some of their deepest insights into what makes people react in predictable ways from experiments conducted on animals and human beings by the internationally famous Russian psychologist, Ivan P. Pavlov. Clifford T. Morgan of Johns Hopkins University, whose *Introduction to Psychology* is a standard textbook in schools and colleges, explains Pavlov's experiments and their interpretations as follows:

> Pavlov's first step was to place food in the mouth of a moderately hungry dog. This normally makes saliva flow. Pavlov called this salivary response to food the *unconditioned response,* because it occurs without any learning, and he called the food the *unconditioned stimulus* for the same reason. His next step was to sound a bell immediately before he presented the food. After pairing the sound of the bell and the offer of food a few times, he noticed that the sound of the bell, without the sight of food, now made the dog salivate. Conditioning had occurred. The bell had become a *conditioned* stimulus, and the flow of saliva had become a *conditioned response* to the bell. In other words, because of the association of food with the sound of the bell, the dog had learned, or become conditioned, to salivate when the bell was sounded. Thus, through conditioning, the bell becomes a stimulus that can evoke a response it never before elicited, namely, salivation.

To confirm his findings that the same technique could be used to unlearn an idea or destroy the conditioned reflex, he reversed the experiment.

> Next Pavlov changed his procedure, sounding the bell *without* presenting the food. The result, after a few trials of this, was that the dog's salivary response became smaller and smaller and finally stopped altogether.

Of course Pavlov didn't *invent* conditioning processes; he discovered them, and his scientific experiments made it possible to understand psychological and physiological factors that have been influencing the behavior pattern of men since the beginning of civilization. Parents have been "conditioning" (in its simplest context) their children for centuries without knowing or caring about the psychological or physiological elements involved.

Nevertheless, the influence of Pavlov on world science has been significant. Although he began his work under the Tsarist regime, at the time of his death in 1936 the Communists had begun to borrow heavily from his experiments for their propaganda activities. Pavlov gave the Russians proof that man can successfully influence and manipulate the complex behavior of human beings.

Pavlov's discoveries relating to conditioned responses, the manner in which a neutral stimulus (such as a bell, a buzzer, a verbal command, a photograph, or an abstract symbol) can become attached to stimuli which normally evoke organic and psychological needs for food and sex, and the emotions of fear or pleasure, etc., have been applied to countless practical situations.

Let us examine the way in which this Pavlovian phenomenon is used in advertising, choosing an example that is familiar to everyone. It has aroused a great deal of controversy concerning taste and appropriateness; nevertheless every "persuader" uses it, although the manner and degree can vary greatly.

First, we can schematize the simple process of conditioning as follows:

1. Expose the subject to the stimulus to which you want him to be conditioned, such as a bell, or a buzzer. In fact, any neutral or seemingly innocuous sound or object. Such sounds or objects are also called the *conditioned stimulus.*

2. Follow this with a stimulus which will naturally call forth a response—such as food, picture of a pretty girl, some form of threat, or something which arouses fear. This is called the *unconditioned stimulus.*

3. With successive repetitions of the sound of the buzzer *and* presentation of food, or the threat of danger, we will soon observe that merely sounding the buzzer will elicit the response appropriate to the food, or the threat—the unconditioned stimulus.

In other words, we can now substitute the buzzer for the actual effective stimulus; and merely sounding the buzzer will, for a time, be a sufficient stimulus for calling forth the response of hunger or fear.

This simple outline has undergone many variations and elaborations over the years, but it serves as a basis for understanding the impact of conditioned responses in the following example of a television commercial for a cough remedy. The sequence might run this way:

1. Loud sound and image of man coughing, repeated many times, filling the screen with no reference to any product. (This amounts to the presentation of both the conditioned and unconditioned stimuli.)

2. Description and visualization of the dangers of coughing. (This reinforces the development of the unconditioned response—fear.)

3. Presentation of the product designed to relieve the fear. (This actually involves the creation of an overlapping conditioning sequence, with the product now being associated with safety.)

4. Modified presentation of coughing, this time tied into safety rather than fear so that coughing will bring out thoughts of the product, rather than thoughts of fear.

With a television commercial, which deals more with probability rather than predictability, not every viewer will react in the same way. That is, there is no control on viewer attention in the home, no control over the need for products demonstrated on TV, and no attempt to preselect audiences by sex, age, physical condition, etc. The television messages are "distributed" in a random manner in the hope of finding appropriate audiences for the message strictly on a probability basis.

In the laboratory an "experimental" sequence of stimulation such as described above could be controlled so as to "fix" the ultimate aim of an association between the cough and the product.

This example is not an isolated instance. One commercial for a breath sweetener makes use of a sound and visual representation standing for "bad breath" (evoking fear), and offers hope in the form of a product designed to assuage fear by destroying bad breath. As the visual devices representing "bad breath" are destroyed, safety becomes associated with the product. Certain headache remedies also follow this type of conditioning sequence.

Sometimes the use of the Pavlovian techniques in advertising can result in commercials that are irritating and insulting to the viewer. I do not condone this kind of advertising; I believe that a good product, service or idea can be presented tastefully.

These techniques can be used for any purpose by anyone who understands them. We have seen how the Soviets have used them for years to influence nearly all phases of human activity. Human needs and fears—poverty, hunger, the dread of war, the wish for self-determination—provide the unconditioned stimuli. And the key phrases of their propaganda—"Capitalists," "Imperialist Aggressors," "Peace"—are the conditioned stimuli which they use to evoke the conditioned response. What Pavlov described as the "collision between the excitatory and inhibitory processes," the product of *experimental neuroses* (i.e., artificially induced disorientation of behavior), has far-reaching implications for the control of social and political behavior.

The Soviets' use of the technique has been described by Stephan T. Possony of Georgetown University and the Foreign Policy Research Institute of the University of Pennsylvania in the *Stanford Research Institute Journal* (Fourth Quarter 1959):

> Fear ... is the disintegrating factor *par excellence* ... the Communists have laid great stress on terror, violence, and purges, and nowadays have enlisted the specter of nuclear war in their strategy of terror. They usually ob-

tain good results from military threats and movements and from giving the impression that they are willing to go beyond the "brink of war." ...

However, the Communists have added an improvement to the age-old art of inducing fright. Once a phenomenon is understood and its behavior has become predictable, men no longer fear it. A danger that is perceived clearly may become a stimulant for action—a most unwelcome possibility. Consequently, the Communists have adopted the techniques of erecting impenetrable "curtains" and of acting unpredictably and capriciously. They alternate smiles with growls, arrest the innocent and free the guilty, keep prisoners in captivity beyond their terms but release them at any odd moment. ... Deliberately, the impression is being created that one can never know what is going to happen next; even if everything is calm now, the next disturbance may be of unparalleled violence.

Taking their psychological warfare one step further, the Communists have found that people can be motivated into uprisings and demonstrations without being aware that they are serving Communistic propaganda goals.

Using various psychological devices, the Russians trigger predicted reactions in both liberals and conservatives everywhere. They do not confine their efforts to movements that appear to be leftist, but as J. Edgar Hoover said in Document No. 59, released on September 23, 1961:

> ... However vehemently the Communists may campaign for the various proposals which compose the party lines, they are not genuinely interested in "reforms" or improving our society. For the party, reforms are useful only to the extent to which they advance the ultimate revolution. The party regards reforms as temporary, transitional adjustments which can be achieved during a

period when the party has not yet attained sufficient strength to risk direct revolutionary action. . . .

Thus they throw the free world off the track by supporting movements to the extreme left, to the extreme right, pro or con, whichever end will help their immediate goals. I believe that there are a number of people who join extreme rightist movements because they are sincerely concerned with the threat of Communism. I also believe that there are liberals who join extreme leftist movements because they fear the threat of Fascism. The evidence indicates that Soviet propaganda attempts to motivate people who have strong feelings on either side. Wherever a fear exists, or can be aroused, the Communist propagandists are ready to exploit it.

If we consider the applications of Pavlovian theory in a broad perspective, observing how it is regarded and used in Russia and the United States, we can find marked differences. Pavlovian principles of influencing human behavior lie behind all of Russia's political moves within the Soviet Union and its satellites, as well as on an international scale. The Russians are called *realists*—that is, they study cause and effect unemotionally and objectively. They are also called *materialists*—they believe that society and the natural world can be understood and changed by scientific means without recourse to the mystiques of religion or spirituality. Consequently they can apply Pavlovian principles, with confidence and without scruple, to propaganda, the control of subject peoples and international politics. Possible human casualties and the subversion of traditional values do not deter them; they are justified, the Communists say, by Marxist-Leninist goals.

In the United States the deliberate use of Pavlovian techniques to influence human behavior is widely regarded as undesirable, even unethical, detrimental to the dignity of man. The words "manipulation," "motivation," "subliminal," "high pressure," and "hard sell" have invidious connotations among Americans. Pavlovian techniques are used, as is generally known, in some advertising, but they are received with an ambivalent attitude. They are recognized, tolerated, to some extent justified, but we as a nation do not like them and we feel guilty, or else indignant, when they are called to our attention.

A number of years ago our advertising agency was asked by the Anti-Tuberculosis Association to prepare some ads for its prediagnostic campaign urging people to have their lungs examined. The ads we developed included an element of fear; they pointed out the danger of tuberculosis and then the promise of discovery and cure as a result of lung X-rays. When we submitted the ads, an executive of the association exclaimed, "No, that is what the quacks do." We told him that the danger of TB actually existed, and that the examination was the first step in eliminating it; that even though quacks did play on human fears, his organization was not a quack outfit, and it was not wrong for a legitimate one to emphasize a real menace to health and try to eliminate it.

We know that the Communists are using an effective means to promote a quack remedy which they claim will lead to peace and human welfare. We know that the means are effective because we have developed them successfully in our own specialized way, to sell products and even ideas. By not using them to the utmost of our skill as a contermeasure against the ideological assaults of the Soviet Union, we place ourselves at a disadvantage.

By deprecating our skills in selling products and ideas, perhaps we are not as materialistic and competitive as we should be in the areas of propaganda and international relations.

Propaganda, of course, is not enough to show the free world, the uncommitted countries, nor the Soviets themselves what we are and what we mean. We must back it with our example, our political actions, our diplomacy, our entire policy. Our product must live up to our claims for it. Here is our big advantage over the Russians—they are not living up to their promises. In America, if a product does not live up to the claims made for it the buyer can choose not to buy it; often he can return it and select another brand. But if the people of a newly independent or economically undeveloped country "buy" our competitor's product and the Communist way of living, it will turn out to be their last real choice; once they have accepted it, they're stuck, even when they have discovered the truth about it; they can't return it and make another choice. Their very survival is involved; they find themselves so deeply committed that they must continue to accept the Communists' "aid," however disappointing and insufficient, and to follow the Communists' plans, and a rigid, compulsory way of life that was not included in the original bargain.

We on the other hand believe in peace and freedom, and we have a legitimate interest in seeing that they prevail throughout the world. If we use our proven skill to develop an effective propaganda organization and correlate it with every phase of our national policy, we will begin to counteract the Soviet offensive on a vital front.

★ IV ★

U. S. Propaganda,
Then and Now

THE people of a nation never think of their accepted beliefs and traditions as propaganda, and Americans particularly would be a little shocked by such an idea. Yet if we examine the history of the truths which we hold to be self-evident, or accept as revelation, it is easy to see that at one time they were disseminated as propaganda in the strict sense of the word. Otherwise they would never have been accepted.

In general, our citizens regard propaganda as one of the less savory aspects of contemporary civilization, a relatively new phenomenon born of twentieth-century European power politics and alien to our moral tradition. It is considered a wicked instrument of deception that "they"— our authoritarian enemies in several wars—have used to advance their evil aim of world domination, but that we try to avoid, or indulge in only reluctantly when absolutely necessary as a countermeasure.

Many of the people in our government today were young men or boys when America embarked on its crusade to "make the world safe for democracy" in 1917. And as they grew to maturity during those years of World War I, they witnessed the first wide-scale use of propaganda on an organized basis in time of conflict.

Unfortunately, much of the propaganda from both the Allies and the Central Powers was reprehensible, and Americans soon came to look with scorn upon this aspect of warfare. This has had its effect on our attitudes today. Our legislators and government officials have become wary of any proposal that our information agencies disseminate anything but hard facts.

When propaganda was first applied on a broad international scale, intensively and often unscrupulously, during World War I, it acquired a lasting stigma. "In loose, popular usage it meant the next thing to a damn lie," pointed out Will Irwin, who was a U. S. propagandist during that period.

Actually, propaganda has a long and not entirely reprehensible history. The word itself dates back to 1622, when Pope Urban VIII established the Propaganda Fidei, a college in which Roman Catholic priests were educated for the propagation of the faith in missionary work. (The noun "propaganda" was taken directly from the participle of the Latin verb meaning "to transmit, to disseminate, to cause to spread or extend.") What we now know as propaganda was employed for religious purposes long before it received that name. Isaiah, Jeremiah, and the other Hebrew prophets of the Old Testament were indisputably propagandists when they attempted to instill in their audiences a belief in Jehovah and the eventual coming of the Messiah; and what else but a propagandist was the persuasive St. Paul as he promoted the cause of Christianity in his Epistles?

By simple dictionary definition, propaganda is "any organized or concerted effort or movement to spread particular doctrines"; more elaborately, Prof. Harold D. Lasswell in the Encyclopaedia Britannica defines it as "an act of advocacy to editorialize or to select the content of channels of communication for the purpose of influencing attitudes on controversial issues." As such, propaganda does not necessarily represent a distortion of truth. Rather it can be based on selected truths, half-truths, or outright falsehoods, separately or in combination.

"Insidious national or factional propaganda, usually consisting of plain lies or plausibly embellished truth, is probably as old as government," Mr. Irwin said. Military propaganda has been traced as far back as the fifth century B.C. in China; evidence of it has been found in records of the Thirty Years' War, the French Revolution, and the Napoleonic Wars. And political propaganda played a vital part in the early history of the United States.

"In establishing American independence, the pen and the press had a merit equal to that of the sword," wrote David Ramsey, an American historian, in 1789. The colonial patriots made extensive use of oratory, slogans, songs, and printed material to foment opposition to England, while the Stamp Act of 1765, which levied taxes on newspapers as well as other printing trades, spurred the editors to join in advocating rebellion.

In *Common Sense* and the *Crisis* series of essays, Thomas Paine defined for the Colonies their ultimate war aim—total separation from the English monarchy—and effectively countered British bids for peace. According to Gorham Munson, author of *Twelve Decisive Battles of the Mind,* Paine successfully applied two major principles of war propaganda: fixing war guilt absolutely on the enemy, and inspiring a reasonable hope in victory.

The Declaration of Independence served a propaganda purpose. Its principal architect, Thomas Jefferson, called it "an appeal to the tribunal of the world ... to command assent." It was the selling of an idea that mobilized the American Colonies for the battle for independence from English domination: "That all men are created equal; that they are endowed with certain inalienable rights; that among these are life, liberty and the pursuit of happiness." The last phrase, repeated over and over again before it caught on, is perhaps the greatest "selling" proposition of all time; it became a banner under which an intellectual aristocracy and a semiliterate and illiterate population of roughly three million united to achieve a freedom that has virtually changed the world; and it has not yet lost its power to move us. Thirteen years later the French revolutionists used a comparable slogan—"*Liberté! Egalité! Fraternité!*"—to arouse a population of 25 million peasants and bourgeoisie to create the second republic in the Western World.

Later, when the war was won, Alexander Hamilton, John Jay, and James Madison wrote and circulated *The*

Federalist Papers in an effort to "sell" the Constitution to the people of the newly independent states. In a letter from New York to Benjamin Rush in Pennsylvania, Hamilton wrote: "I send you herewith a series of political papers under the denomination of the Federalist, published in favor of the new Constitution. They do good here and it is imagined some of the last numbers may have a good effect upon some of your Quaker members of convention. . . . It might be well to give them a passage . . . to your more Southern neighbors."

Propaganda was scarcely less significant in the Civil War. Lincoln's Emancipation Proclamation of 1863 was, among other things, a propaganda document designed to win support for the Union side at home and abroad, and it followed one of the most influential propaganda publications of all time, the abolitionist *Uncle Tom's Cabin.*

Propaganda has been credited, or blamed, for involving the United States in at least two other wars (and in fact it was not entirely neglected in peacetime; Britain's Pax Britannica and the United States' "Manifest Destiny" were used to justify expansion). The role of the William Randolph Hearst newspaper chain in instigating the Spanish-American War is well documented, and British propaganda is often cited as the single most important factor in our entry into World War I. Historian H. C. Peterson, in *Propaganda for War,* asserted that "propaganda was not only responsible in a large degree for the American entrance into the war, but it was also responsible for the temper and the irrationality of the peace treaty and the vindictiveness of the postwar years."

During World War I, propaganda for the first time was

formalized in comprehensive programs conducted on a large scale by a number of governments, simultaneously and competitively. At the beginning of the war an English philosopher, Benjamin Kidd, issued a remarkably astute prophecy: "The science of creating and transmitting public opinion under the influence of collective emotion is about to become the principal science of civilization, to the mastery of which all governments and all powerful interests will in the future address themselves with every resource at their command."

At the outset of the war, when the U. S. was not yet committed, Germany broadcast slanted news abroad and skillfully utilized German-American organizations, exchange professors, and U. S. offices of German business firms to spread its propaganda in America.

When the United States got into the war in 1917, President Wilson's administration set up the Committee on Public Information with George Creel as chairman, marking this nation's first attempt to use propaganda on an organized basis. Creel characterized its mission as a "fight for the minds of men," believing that "moral verdicts" were as significant as military decisions. With a net expenditure of less than five million dollars, the Creel Committee, as it came to be known, conducted a full-scale propaganda operation on both the domestic and foreign fronts. It distributed news and feature material, photographs, cartoons and films; produced advertisements, pamphlets, and specialized publications; and sponsored lectures, parades, exhibits of captured war matériel, and special activities directed to women and the foreign-born. Aside from its primary goal—to arouse support for the

Allied war effort—the Committee also supervised "voluntary" censorship.

Almost continuously until Congress abolished it abruptly in 1919, the Committee was the target of heated controversy, for propaganda had already become a suspect art. Outright propagandizing of the American people was viewed with resentment and suspicion in many quarters, and such activities as promoting war relief for the Allies were criticized as "orgies of idealism and ballyhoo." Congressional committees investigated accusations of partisanship, inaccuracy, dishonesty, and inefficiency. Moreover, President Wilson was lukewarm in his support of the agency and of propaganda in general. Ironically his declaration of U. S. war aims in the celebrated "Fourteen Points" proved to be a master stroke of propaganda.

Despite his difficulties, Creel's confidence remained unshaken. He wrote, in 1920:

> Under the pressure of tremendous necessities an organization grew that not only reached deep into every American community, but that carried to every corner of the civilized globe the full message of America's idealism, unselfishness and indomitable purpose. We fought prejudice, indifference, and disaffection at home, and we fought ignorance and falsehood abroad. We strove for the maintenance of our own morale and the Allied morale by every process of stimulation; every possible expedient was employed to break through the barrage of lies that kept the people of the Central Powers in darkness and delusion; we sought the friendship and support of the neutral nations by continuous presentation of the facts. We did not call it propaganda, for that word, in German hands, had come to be associated with deceit and corruption. Our effort was educational and informative through-

out, for we had such confidence in our case as to feel that no other argument was needed than the simple, straightforward presentation of facts.

After the Armistice, George Sylvester Viereck, a pro-German propagandist in America before 1917, said, "The World War proved to be a postgraduate course for propagandists." Propaganda flourished partly because of the growth of communications, and the rising educational level in Europe and the United States. "The field of propaganda widens as illiteracy disappears."

Between the two world wars the United States again was without an official propaganda agency or program. Six months after the attack on Pearl Harbor, President Franklin D. Roosevelt created the Office of War Information, but because of a jurisdictional dispute with the Office of Strategic Services, it was not until March 1943 that the OWI began full operation.

Basically its activities, under Director Elmer Davis, a newsman, paralleled those of the Creel Committee with a Domestic Branch and an Overseas Operations Branch. But again Congressional attacks soon reduced the Domestic Branch to impotence. Although the Overseas Branch also was sharply criticized, and wracked by internal strife, an organization was gradually built up with recruits from the communications industry and attained some degree of efficiency. The Voice of America initiated worldwide radio broadcasts; "outposts" were established in leading cities of Allied and neutral countries to propagandize through local media; and psychological warfare was waged in the European and Far Eastern theaters, using radio and front-line loudspeakers, as well as leaflets air-dropped or fired in artillery shells, to demoralize enemy troops and induce surrender.

At the war's end the OWI was transferred to the State Department under an order from President Truman, who said, "The nature of present-day foreign relations makes it essential for the United States to maintain informational activities abroad as an integral part of the conduct of our foreign affairs."

But neither the State Department nor Congress showed much interest in peacetime propaganda, and the program languished until the emerging struggle with Soviet Communism became starkly apparent to a group of Congressmen journeying overseas in the summer of 1947. When Congress reconvened in January 1948, it passed the Smith-Mundt Act, described as "the first formal Congressional act authorizing the United States Government to try to influence the opinions of other peoples in a planned, systematic, and continuing fashion."

With the objective of promoting a better understanding of the United States in other countries, the Act (Public Law 402) provided for "an information service to disseminate abroad information about the United States, its people and policies promulgated by the Congress, the President, the Secretary of State and other responsible officials of government having to do with matters affecting foreign affairs." The State Department was instructed to rely primarily on private media in providing this service, and one of its first moves was to contract with broadcasting companies for an overseas broadcasting service to present "a full and fair picture" of the United States.

By early 1950, after the first Soviet atomic explosion, it

was obvious that something more than a defensive, long-range program of this kind was needed. Following a recommendation of the National Security Council for an expanded propaganda offensive, President Truman called for "a great Campaign of Truth" to persuade people throughout the world to line up with us on the side of freedom.

Meanwhile, the military services, impressed by the results of psychological warfare in World War II, brought pressure for a part in the foreign information program. The upshot of the Defense Department's battle with the State Department was a 1951 executive order creating a high-level planning and coordinating body called the Psychological Strategy Board, composed of representatives of the two departments and of the Central Intelligence Agency.

The Board proved relatively ineffective. But the foreign information program grew, particularly in the Voice of America and the Overseas Information Center operations. At the same time other organizations, such as the Mutual Security Agency, the Technical Cooperation Administration, and the Defense Department, were conducting information programs of their own. Assistant Secretary of State Edward W. Barrett tried to coordinate and consolidate these duplicating operations, with limited success.

In 1952, Dr. George Gallup, whose Gallup Polls have worldwide recognition, declared: "If I were to cite my chief criticism of our propaganda efforts of the last ten years, it would be that we have never followed the simple rule of selling ideas one at a time; we say one thing today, another tomorrow."

The next move to bring order out of the growing chaos

was the creation in 1952 of a semi-autonomous International Information Administration within the State Department. It was to receive policy guidance from the Assistant Secretary of State but have a free hand in operations.

Dr. Wilson Compton, who was appointed to head the IIA, soon found that semi-autonomy left much to be desired. His predicament can be indicated by this extract from the February 1953 report of the U. S. Advisory Commission on Information, a watchdog group that Congress had established in the Smith-Mundt Act:

> There has been a singular lack of enthusiasm and imagination in the [State] Department's development of the information program. When the program was first set up under Department of State auspices it got off to a slow and unconvincing start. There was much overt and covert opposition to it in the Department. Instead of initiating and carrying on a fresh, dynamic program, the Department converted it into a low-level and secondary operation. It soon became apparent that the Department was more interested in conforming the information program to its own long-established conventions than in carrying out the Congressional intention of Public Law 402.
>
> Repeated recommendations of our commission were disregarded or reluctantly and half-heartedly adopted. Such progress as has been made has followed only after repeated recommendations, protests, and threats of reduced appropriations.

The five-member Advisory Commission, headed by an educator, Dr. Mark A. May of Yale University, made one of three searching examinations of the foreign information program after the change of Administration in January 1953. The other inquiries were conducted by President

Eisenhower's Committee on Foreign Information Activities and the Hickenlooper Subcommittee of the Senate Foreign Relations Committee.

Acting upon their recommendations (and the desire of Secretary of State John Foster Dulles to have all operational programs removed from the State Department), President Eisenhower on August 1, 1953, consolidated all foreign information programs and operations in a new, independent United States Information Agency, responsible to him through the National Security Council.

The USIA director was made a member of the new Operations Coordinating Board, which replaced the old Psychological Strategy Board and was intended to coordinate more effectively all instruments of foreign policy. USIA shifted the emphasis on the information program from Washington headquarters to the field. USIA officers overseas were to be subordinate to the State Department's chiefs of mission, and at home the Department was to provide policy guidance for the Agency.

President Eisenhower described the USIA's purpose in these words: "To submit evidence to peoples of other nations by means of communications techniques that the objectives and policies of the United States are in harmony with and will advance their legitimate aspirations for freedom, progress, and peace."

This purpose was to be carried out "by explaining and interpreting to foreign peoples the objectives and policies of the United States Government by depicting imaginatively the correlation between United States policies and the legitimate aspirations of other peoples in the world; by unmasking and countering hostile attempts to distort or to frustrate the objectives and policies of the United States; and by delineating those important aspects of life and culture of the people of the United States which facilitate understanding of the policies and objectives of the Government of the United States."

Theodore C. Streibert, former chairman of the Mutual Broadcasting Company, was named first director of the USIA, and he promised to "concentrate on objective, factual news reporting the appropriate commentaries, designed to present a full exposition of important United States actions and policies, especially as they affect individual countries and areas. . . . In presenting facts we shall see to it that they are not distorted and that their selection does not misrepresent a given situation."

The output of the USIA was to be dignified, straightforward, credible, and convincing. Apparently, however, the agency in its day-to-day operations showed signs of behaving like a propaganda unit, because Streibert's successors—Arthur Larson, a lawyer, economist and author who stayed only one year, and George V. Allen, a career service officer—changed the USIA's approach during the 1957–60 period.

"Briefly, the Agency shift in approach meant the elimination of polemics from its broadcasts and written output," the staff director of the Advisory Commission has explained, in typical official-ese. "Further, it meant the careful and scrupulous regard for a truthful and balanced account of events that were occurring in the United States and abroad which the communications specialist considered pertinent for dissemination abroad."

It is interesting to note that the recent USIA director,

Edward R. Murrow, who came in with the Kennedy administration in 1961, viewed his assignment this way: "The business of my agency is to make the policy of this country as designed by the President everywhere intelligible, and wherever possible, palatable. It is fundamental that we operate on the basis of truth. Ours is, and must be, a dedication to the factual. . . . Our objective is, and must be credibility."

This is, of course, the view of a newspaperman; but Mr. Murrow's view of his agency's job seemed narrower than that envisioned by President Eisenhower in 1953.

Carl T. Rowan, successor to Edward R. Murrow, has indicated that he is following his predecessor's guidelines. When Mr. Rowan took his oath of office President Johnson said, "My only admonition is to tell the truth."

Carl Rowan's response was, "Mr. President, that is all I know how to do." Certainly, no one would object to this point of view in any activity dealing with people. The question is, do news and news headlines—which news-oriented men deal with—reflect the truth about our nation?

USIA operated on a budget of about $134,000,000 for fiscal 1964.

Here is a summary of USIA's report on its activities:

It has about 12,000 employes, including some 7,500 citizens of countries in which the USIA operates. Of the 4,500 Americans in USIA, some 3,000 work in the U. S. and 1,500 overseas.

The press and publications service operates an international broadcast service that distributes about 10,000 words of news daily to 89 posts abroad which interpret and distribute the information for local use. "Canned" feature material, texts of U. S. policy statements, posters, pamphlets, and cartoons are also made available to 2,700 foreign publications. Four slick magazines—in Russian, Polish, Spanish, and Arabic—are produced in Washington, while 68 other magazines in 25 languages, as well as 20 newspapers, are published overseas.

The Information Center service has 176 libraries, 85 reading rooms, and 128 binational centers abroad. More than a million people in 55 countries have taken English-teaching courses in these facilities. About 2½ million books are circulated, and additional millions of books are distributed to individuals and institutions annually. Traveling exhibits, lectures, and seminars are also sponsored by these outposts.

The motion picture service produces documentaries, newsreels, and short subjects for showing in theatres, at the information centers, on television, and by mobile film units to an audience estimated at 600 million persons a month. Over 200 film libraries in 98 countries each contain 500 to 1,000 foreign-language films.

The television service furnishes over 500 kinescopes and video tapes annually to stations in 57 countries serving about 55 million television sets.

Also under the USIA's wing is the Voice of America. In addition to providing recorded feature material to foreign radio stations, the Voice broadcasts in 37 languages to an average daily audience exceeding 20 million persons. Its 730 hours a week are about equal to Communist China's broadcast time, and far below the Soviet Union's more than 1,000 hours of direct international programing. Furthermore, jamming by Communist nations' 2,000 interference transmitters keeps a varying proportion of Voice broadcasts from getting through to the intended audience.

Under Mr. Murrow's direction, USIA first began to show some signs of trying to catch up with the Communists in reaching the millions of people whose decision on whether to choose Communism or the West will eventually play a major role in the present Cold War struggle.

USIA has increased its Spanish-language broadcasts to Latin America by 50 percent, and opened 27 new libraries in Africa in 1961 alone. And commenting on USIA's news service, *Printers' Ink* said: "Instead of diffuse, general, and often haphazard coverage, USIA now gives considerable emphasis to themes of positive propaganda values."

USIA is rightfully proud of its efforts in covering the space flight of the U.S. astronauts, the story of the Berlin Wall, and its extensive job of reporting on the Cuban crisis of 1962. The Berlin Wall story was especially effective, since USIA tagged it the "Wall of Shame," and stuck to one central theme—the wall was a sign of defeat for Communism.

Yet the fundamental criticism that the U. S. propaganda program is long on information but short on persuasion is still valid.

The influential French newspaper *Le Monde* considers the Voice of America programs beamed to Europe "too prudent, too official, too conformist." According to *Le Monde's* correspondent in Poland, Voice efforts to avoid offending the Gomulka regime have cost it many listeners. In some Communist satellite countries, Radio Free Europe claims a larger share of the audience because it uses a more aggressive approach.

The USIA still lacks a positive, coherent, and comprehensive approach to the task which has been assigned to it; and it lacks the personnel and the funds to carry it out. It has often complained that its annual budget is less than the amount a leading soap manufacturer in this country spends to advertise its products. This is a sad fact, particularly in view of the billions which the Russians spend on their propaganda machine.

Any alteration of policy or increase in appropriations must be undertaken by Congress and the entire executive branch of the government as well as the top brass of the USIA. It is the President and his advisers who finally determine what USIA should do, and the Congress which, by laws and appropriations, can retard or advance any USIA project. Congress has borne the brunt of the blame for an inadequate budget; but the executive branch has not pressed as hard as it might have to help USIA.

In the past, USIA has not been a particular favorite with Mr. Johnson. As a Senator, he rode herd on its appropriations with a cautious eye and cut some $5,000,000 from its current budget request, according to reports. With little visible support from the White House, USIA officials year after year troop over to the Capitol at budget time to ask for their money. There, Congressmen ask them some searching questions about the effectiveness of the USIA. Apparently the answers are not compelling enough to elicit a vote of confidence, or a larger budget for the Agency.

Senator J. William Fulbright, chairman of the Foreign

Relations Committee, recently told his colleagues: "I have great difficulty in finding any very favorable reaction to the Voice of America, but that is a matter of opinion. I supported that program, too, but I do not have any great faith in it."

Let us look at the achievements of the USIA, with a view to suggesting two ways of improving our propaganda objectives: placing emphasis on persuasion rather than merely the dissemination of information; and enlisting the services of men and women trained in the arts of persuasion.

Is Our Strategy Effective?

WHAT are we getting for the money spent on USIA? Can it be proved that extensive cultural programs are worth the money in winning friends for the United States? Why does USIA stress the teaching of English language in its overseas posts while the Russians pass out local language dictionaries with politically slanted definitions? Why is *Free World Magazine* (published in seven different editions) described as "hard-hitting" when, for example, the November 1961 issue contains a lot about Asia's growth and about the birth of a chicken and the wool-growing industry in Korea? Why are there not articles that hit hard at Communism or at least are pro-American?

These are the questions asked by Congressmen at budget hearings on the USIA, and they suggest that the USIA needs personnel versed in the arts of persuasion to plead its case in Congress as well as throughout the free world.

The USIA, in seeking people to tell our story abroad,

generally turns to the field of journalism. According to Herb McGussion, deputy director of public information in the Agency, its editorial and press staff is "made up primarily of men who are graduates of wire services and newspapers in the United States." Clearly this is the policy of the USIA. In addition one finds men who have been broadcasters, educators and research specialists; but of the top eighteen men in the USIA, *only one* has had any experience in the art of persuasion—that is, in advertising —and that man spent only one year in an advertising agency.

There is no question of the responsibility and dedication of the men who staff the upper echelons of the USIA. Some of them gave up prominent positions and good incomes to work for the government. Many of them have extensive backgrounds in foreign affairs and invaluable knowledge of certain areas of the world. But they are not trained in the art of persuasion. Journalism and scholarship are not enough for the task of projecting the image of America in foreign countries.

Some advertising people have been or are in the USIA, but most of them are shunted to the Office of Private Cooperation, which works with the business community to supplement USIA activities. While this is worthwhile work, it does not permit advertising men to use their knowledge at the policy-making and executive level. Two exceptions might be noted. Leland S. Briggs of the McCann-Erickson agency was Chief of Press Services in the mid-50's, and Leonard F. Erickson, also of McCann-Erickson, directed the Voice of America during the same period. Unfortunately, as we have seen, the administration soon clamped down on USIA's attempt to expand its propaganda techniques, apparently preferring the "straight news" approach.

Others advertising men have served in advisory capacities, including Sigurd S. Larmon, former board chairman of the Young & Rubicam agency, who still serves on the USIA Advisory Committee. But after conversations with executives of USIA and Mr. Larmon, I doubt whether the Advisory Committee has very much influence in the operation of USIA.

Several people with public relations experience serve in USIA, and it is a common mistake of people outside of the field of advertising to consider that advertising men and public relations men are in the same "line of work." It is true that both attempt to persuade, but the methods are vastly different. A public relations man who wants to bring his message to the great mass of people must get "free" space or air time in the mass media. His science, which often makes great contributions to the success of a campaign, is the science of fitting his message to the needs of the medium so that it will be used, and his effectiveness depends on the whims of the editors and broadcasters. He may have to use a "gimmick"—such as a picture of a pretty model holding the product—in order to get the publicity, and the gimmick may well overshadow the message. Or his well-conceived campaign may end up in the editor's wastebasket or find its way into marginal publications.

In the public relations approach, based on free space, you cannot be sure of any sort of continuity or repetition of your message, which is vital to implanting ideas.

In the advertising approach, on the other hand, the print space or broadcast time is purchased. The advertising man makes a science of choosing just the right words and placing them in just the right media, at the proper time, for maximum effectiveness. He has absolute control over the content of the message, and he can repeat it as often as he thinks necessary. Paying for the space can be expensive, but when compared to the cost of the more conventional Cold War weapons, the use of paid space or time by our government to sell our ideals to the world would be money well spent.

Publicity can be a vital adjunct to any campaign, but straightforward messages such as those used in advertising are a necessary core because they provide the continuity and repetition of message which is essential to successful mass persuasion. And as a final point—while publishers and editors generally are careful to avoid pressure from advertisers, they are more likely to be impressed with our government if we pay our own way in the matter of presenting our message. And when they are approached with publicity material, the chances of acceptance are that much better.

It is easy to see why USIA staffs itself with newsmen and newswomen. Official Washington and the press are on intimate terms. Government officials have a close relationship with members of the press, and the press in turn regards Washington as its lifeline.

Members of the press maintain friendships among government officials to improve their news sources. The politicians maintain their association with newsmen for the purpose of getting information to their constituents.

On the other hand, it is quite likely that neither the top men at USIA, nor top men in government posts and Congress, come in close contact with advertising men. It is doubtful that these men understand the skills of advertising people.

Since the USIA is staffed largely with ex-newsmen, it is inevitable that news of what goes on in our country should be the vehicle for United States propaganda abroad.

One important difference between advertising and journalism—between copywriting and news writing—is the type of reaction generally elicited by each. The end toward which the techniques and practices of advertising aim is to induce people to action. On the other hand, news stories usually call for no action. The news story usually gives the facts about a certain event or occurrence or tells what is happening in a certain situation. After reading this news there is generally nothing for a person to do. Granted, the reader may think about or talk about it and feel deeply about what he has read. But the objective news story is not supposed to overtly call for action. The main purpose of this news is to inform, not to elicit action.

On the other hand, a good advertising campaign, thoroughly researched and creatively executed, moves people to action; if it is successful, people will buy the product or the service.

News deals largely with current events. These events change hourly, which keeps people both interested and coming back for more news constantly. The tremendous development of the news-on-the-hour programs is an example of how often people want to know what is happening. News does not have to sell or be sold; most people seek the news.

A particularly striking news story might be remembered for a while, but this doesn't mean that there is any sort of personal commitment to the story. Because news is transitory, little of what is read or heard is retained for long. Because it is constantly being replaced by other, fresher news, most people don't remember for a very long time much of what they read or hear in the news.

In his *Introduction to Psychology*, Clifford T. Morgan describes a number of experiments in "Learning and Remembering." After studying these various experiments, one can only conclude that even after some material is studied a number of times, as much as 90 percent of what is read and heard is forgotten within 24 hours.

In order for people to retain ideas, the ideas must not only be defined in very simple terms, but must be repeated over and over again, usually in association with something they are personally interested in.

Thus, the techniques of persuasion must include devices for drawing attention and repeating a message over and over. People rarely seek out advertising, except for classified ads and retail store price advertising; it is necessary to bring its products and ideas to their notice, and keep on doing it year after year. The same principle applies to propaganda. It's obvious that news cannot serve this purpose.

Edward R. Murrow, a respected newsman, said, when he was director of the USIA, "We must persuade, or perish in the attempt." He recognized the need to persuade; but there is little in the output of the USIA that resembles persuasion in the sense that I have emphasized; and a subsequent statement by Murrow indicated that his idea of persuasion is vastly different from an advertising man's. He said:

> We operate on the basis of truth. Voice of America news broadcasts are balanced and objective. They cover all the news, even when it hurts. American traditions and American ethics require us to be truthful, but the most important reason is that truth is the best propaganda and lies are the worst. To be persuasive we must be believable; to be believable we must be credible; to be credible we must be truthful. It is as simple as that.

Unfortunately, it is *not* that simple. While it is true that believability is vital to persuasiveness, it is a mistake to equate news with truth.

The truth is not always news, and the news is not always true. And that is one dangerous flaw in the news-oriented propaganda program.

News often does not convey truth in its larger sense. News is made up of the unusual things that happen, and thus may not reflect a true picture of the people or places in the news. But by committing themselves to broadcasting "all the news," USIA is forced to broadcast around the world news of race riots, political scandals and other events which give a partial and hence distorted picture of life in these United States. Is *this* broadcasting the "truth"?

Further, in this era of swift communications, news services have come to regard speed in reporting almost as an end in itself, and accuracy is bound to suffer at times. If a news item is inaccurate, or quotes someone who later turns out to have been lying, or tells only one side of the story, it may nonetheless be considered as important news. Thus USIA, under its "all the news" banner, must carry it. Is *this* broadcasting the "truth"?

The danger of this rush to compete with regular news services was evident at the time of the assassination of President Kennedy. First USIA reports said the assassination occurred in Dallas, which it identified as the scene of recent right-wing demonstrations, implying that right-wing extreme elements were responsible for the deed. Radio Moscow quickly and gleefully recounted the USIA broadcast. And even though cooler heads at USIA deleted the right-wing reference in subsequent broadcasts, the damage had been done.

Such about-faces are tough enough for a commercial news medium which often must sacrifice accuracy for speed. But it is inexcusable for an official spokesman for the United States Government to act in such haste that it causes international repercussions.

The free flow of news is vital to our free society. But much news is concerned with the atypical and does not lend itself to a program of presenting a balanced picture of the United States.

This news "trap" deepens further with the assumption that the *significance* of the news event will be understood by the listener or reader. Let me illustrate. USIA might try to justify the reporting of racial demonstrations in this country on the grounds that it demonstrates our freedom of speech in action. But the news itself, being spectacular, almost always overshadows the significance behind it. It would be better to precondition the audience in advance or wait until the event has passed; then, with the excitement over, explain how the event fits into the fabric of our free society.

If the aim of the USIA is to increase American prestige abroad by giving a balanced picture of life in the United States, then the unrestricted broadcast of topical news is not bringing about the desired result. We have crime, violence, poverty and injustice, corruption and scandal like any other country; but they are not the aspects of American life of which we are proud, and if we are trying to make a good impression we do not emphasize our faults. In advertising we admittedly stress the positive benefits of a product, service or idea; and there is hardly one that does not have its faults if we chose to seek them out. Usually the negative aspects are unimportant compared to the positive benefits. If our avowed intention is to make friends abroad, then there is no advantage in putting our worst foot forward.

We have racial problems, which are covered fully in our free press. The wire services send this news around the world, and our own Voice of America does the same. Thus people abroad, in neutral or newly independent countries, are made aware that we have racial problems—but not that we have a free press and free speech. The same people then read or hear carefully controlled news from Communist countries, which tell of our race problems but not of their own. These readers and listeners notice the absence of news of race problems in Communist countries, but they are not reminded that all the news emanating from Communist countries is government-controlled and sedulously biased.

The whole idea of a totally government-controlled press

and radio is repugnant to a free society—United States citizens would not tolerate it in this country; the Constitution protects us against it. I am not suggesting that the USIA should broadcast distorted accounts of news. *I am suggesting that it get out of the news business completely and leave it to the free press.* The government can, of course, in any free country make statements in its own behalf and release information to the press—and that is all that a government should do in the way of disseminating straight news.

It is said that news is a powerful propaganda medium, and it is true that a news story dramatically told may have a widespread effect; news has been known to create momentary havoc. It was reported recently that two people died after eating a can of spoiled tuna, and sales of tuna dropped by ten million cans despite the fact that a billion cans are consumed each year and for forty years not one person died. Thousands of people got rid of their dogs when a few people were bitten by a dog suspected of having rabies. Parents all over the country have been panicked into keeping their children home from school because of a kidnapping in a faraway city. Spotlessly clean and disease-free Switzerland lost an important part of its tourist business because of a typhoid epidemic in only one skiing resort.

One might argue that such results from newspaper publicity show that news is a powerful tool for selling. But the results of these stories were only temporary—tuna sales returned to normal after several months, people continue buying dogs for pets, and children attend school as usual.

The unusual or spectacular ideas in connection with

these events go into the mind very quickly—probably much more quickly than a regular advertising message, which is dull by comparison. But these ideas leave the mind just as rapidly because of the way the human memory mechanism works. The idea that is put into people's minds continuously is the one that remains the longest. People are not necessarily consciously aware of such an idea, but repetition can establish it so strongly in the subconscious that it may take a long time to leave the mind, if it leaves at all.

News does not lend itself to repetition. No matter how spectacular a news story is, there is virtually no permanent or long-term effect. And incidentally, advertising that depends on the spectacular for its effect is not always successful either. This type of advertising doesn't "wear" as well under frequent repetition as a message delivered "straight" or in a simple, entertaining manner.

News is relative; nearly everything that happens in the news is repeated many times in many places, but those events that make the news are there because of the circumstances of that day. A news story that might make the headlines on one day may not even be covered on another day. There are race riots, robberies, murders and political scandals happening all over the world daily, but some may never get into the news, either because no one was there to get the story; because some other, more important, event overshadowed it; or because of an individual's editorial judgment.

Often when one incident is reported in the news, a series of similar events are reported all over the country—which indicates that these events were happening frequently but did not become newsworthy until one important story put all such events in the news. When a flying saucer is reported in one area, similar stories arise throughout the country. The point here is that people may have hallucinations of seeing flying objects frequently, but their experience does not become newsworthy until one incident gets into the news.

Thus news, as a means of conveying an impression of the texture of life in America, is haphazard—our daily experience does not consist entirely of murder, riots, scandal, flying saucers.

News is exciting to work with, especially if it is sensational, just as well-founded gossip of a sensational kind is more interesting than the more important round of daily affairs. There are many more happy marriages than divorces, but the divorces make the news. News reporters attempt to be impartial, which is proper, and good reporters are; but newsmen are often tempted to seek out the sensational to attract readers. I recall in my early career, when I was training to become circulation manager of a Hearst paper, my superior and I were watching a water show at the end of Navy Pier in Chicago. Fifteen thousand spectators were crowded into a small area. My boss said, with enthusiasm, "Wouldn't it make a great story and sell a hell of a lot of papers if this pier suddenly sank?"

A common tag line in news and publicity circles is "Praise me if you can, damn me if you must, but for heaven's sake, please don't ignore me." The concept of publicity which underlies this remark might benefit a circus or a sideshow or a movie star. People may like to see or read something shocking and revolting, but they would not place their trust in a nation that has a revolting or shocking image. When news broadcasts feature the less savory aspects of our national life, they do not promote our interests abroad.

The Voice of America wastes much of its valuable time, personnel and facilities in broadcasting news that has little relation to the image of America that we are trying to create.

This is not to say that the USIA should stop putting out *all* information. If it were decided that the world should know the government's position on a certain matter, USIA should broadcast that information. If Red propagandists tell lies about an important news event, the USIA should give its version in answer. And if a particular event had value to us as news, USIA should cooperate with the world press in getting out the story. It should concentrate on delivering messages that are carefully calculated to promote our aims. Cooperation with private news media in supplying information on special events, such as U. S. space shots, is certainly appropriate. Otherwise, its program should not be determined by the news of the day but rather by the messages it wants to get across to foreign countries. It can act as the government's press bureau by releasing official reports of the government's activities to world news organizations, but the broadcasting of straight news is a waste of time. The free world is already serviced by many non-governmental news-gathering agencies, and Radio Free Europe broadcasts behind the Iron Curtain. The USIA need not duplicate these functions.

The USIA's radio, the Voice of America, should devote its resources and personnel to carrying out what is called in advertising an "institutional campaign," a consistent and carefully planned program that gives a constructive view of our society, and one that would, over a period of time, bring to foreign peoples a steady, controlled presentation of our sales message—the ideas of peace and freedom.

We know that American entertainment is so popular abroad that in itself it can build goodwill for us; and it attracts large audiences. We should make use of entertainment programs to attract listeners in the same way that advertisers do. Along with such programs there should be brief, clearly identified, persuasive messages to condition people to understand our aims. These messages, of course, would have to be repeated many times to become effective.

This procedure is one that the professional advertising man is trained to follow. He uses it every day for selling products; and he could use the same skills in helping us to sell our ideas abroad.

The Voice of America also broadcasts commentaries on the news, and theoretically these might be more effective than the broadcasting of news. But let's look at the actual programs. I have examined many of the scripts produced by USIA for transmission overseas. Here are some examples:

> In one of our previous broadcasts we examined some of the political and theoretical considerations that seem to have been instrumental in triggering the massive campaign currently conducted by the Communists against the Common Market and European integration. Politically, the Common Market appears to affect adversely Communist strategy and tactics since it contributes most successfully to the political and economic stabilization of Western Europe. By promoting social justice and eco-

nomic prosperity it denies the Communists the opportunity to exploit poverty and discontent. It also deals a serious blow to Communist theories since it abolishes some of the basic tenets of the Marxist and Leninist doctrines. Contrary to these doctrines, developments in the Common Market countries demonstrate that in highly industrialized countries the poor do not get poorer; the small bourgeois do not become proletarians; and competition between economically powerful national states tends to produce mutually beneficial cooperation and not, as Lenin predicted, "a bloody morass of imperialist wars."

A Voice of America news analyst had this to say about Cuba:

> The acquisition of modern weaponry, together with large increments in conventional armaments, do imply a substantial increase in Cuba's military power, especially relative to the other neighboring Latin-American countries. However, at present, Cuba's military posture appears to be essentially defensive in nature.

The language of these scripts is so turgid and the ideas so abstract that they could only appeal to a minute fraction of the listeners of any country; the majority could not possibly be attracted by such broadcasts or understand their significance, no matter how eager they might be for information. Certainly no advertiser could hope to sell his wares with this kind of jargon.

The Voice of America feature programs cover such topics as "The New Wave in American Movies," "National Institute of Arts and Letters," "Eugene O'Neill: Part I," "A Family Portrait," "Earthquakes: Cause and Effect" and "Dead Horse, the Featherbed and Unwork"—the latter being a discussion of useless work in our society of super-abundance!

If American broadcasts are to achieve interest and believability, and reach wide audiences and bring about action, then the USIA must devise programs of far broader appeal. And a part of a broadcast time should be used for direct messages, day in, day out, repeating the central theme of our campaign and exposing the lies of Soviet propaganda.

I have spoken of the ideas and the image of itself that the United States wants to propagate abroad as "products," and of the techniques of persuasion as "selling." As an advertising man I am, of course, aware of the bias against commercial advertising that exists among government officials, educators and laymen; and I have heard many times the stereotyped objection that "you can't sell democracy like soap flakes."

The USIA and its high officials acknowledge that their task is persuasion, and they use the terminology of advertising to describe it, even though they shy away from the idea. Edward R. Murrow has said: "We articulate and distribute, not advertising for cigarettes and soap, but clarification of government policy and deeds."

And another ex-newsman, now a top executive of the USIA, Thomas C. Sorensen, deputy director of the USIA for policy and plans, speaking to the Direct Mail Advertising Assn. even likened the USIA to an advertising agency. He described the "client"—United States of America; "product"—peaceful world; and "market"—the 2,800,000,000 people in foreign countries. He also said that the competition (Communism) is advertising to the same market.

Speaking of the results of the USIA's selling effort, Mr. Sorensen said:

> Like you, we seek action as the end product of persuasion. But we are without the handy index of sales volume to know how we are succeeding. No cash register rings when a man changes his mind. No computer clicks when a vision of freedom crosses a mind somewhere. No financial page carries the rise or fall of confidence in an ideal. No rating service says the campaign is successful when a hope turns into a consensus. We only know we've succeeded when people act for freedom, act to broaden their range of choice, act to improve their lot without sacrificing their independence.

Strip away the rhetoric from the foregoing paragraph and this fact emerges: USIA does not know if it is succeeding in its appointed task until it is too late.

Only when people act, Mr. Sorensen says, do we know if our propaganda effort has been effective. If they act the way we'd hoped, all well and good. If they act contrary to our wishes, it's too late for propaganda.

This view does not show a very firm grasp of the uses of research to determine results. People do not change their attitudes or behavior overnight. Research, if it is conducted intelligently and continually, can indicate trends in the results of a selling campaign, and if there are changes, favorable or otherwise, creative measures can be taken at the proper time. The use of research is vital, albeit costly, in any advertising campaign. The USIA spends very little to find out how effective its messages are. According to Congressional testimony, $381,171 was budgeted for this purpose in fiscal 1964.

It is clear that the USIA does not do for its client—the U.S.A.—what an advertising agency does for its client; and Mr. Murrow and Mr. Sorensen do not use the terms "persuasion," "client," and "market" with the same meaning as an advertising man does. And certainly any advertising man, if he were trying to persuade people to accept our way of life, would not use the same terms or even the same methods he would use to sell cigarettes or soap. But he would know that fundamentally he is working with the same mental processes in the people he is trying to reach whether he is selling ideas or cigarettes.

There is another way, and an important one, in which the USIA could benefit from the services of the advertising industry. Like many another government agency, it must deal with the constantly recurring problem of how to get from Congress sufficient funds to carry on its work. If advertising men occupied positions of authority in the agency, they could use their skill in persuasion to present to Congress an effective picture of the task which the USIA must accomplish to counter the Soviet propaganda assault. Congressmen want to know what the USIA can do for the country, and they want to be able to give their constituents a true account of the Agency's mission, and what it does for the money appropriated to its use. Men with advertising experience can be useful to both the Agency and Congress by presenting the problem in terms that will make sense to the legislator and to his constituents. If a Congressman can show voters how he has helped the country by approving a substantial increase in the USIA budget, he will be more likely to back the increase.

In 1961, advertising agency president Leo Burnett spoke

to a group of advertising men about USIA, and noted that USIA has "gradually been strangled for lack of money and facilities." And he added: "Certainly it is time that America woke up to the fact that unless this battle is won, nothing else will count. As lamentable as is the lack of funds, I advance the point of view that a reinvigorated effort to sell our system and the democratic principles of Western civilization could well make use of some good advertising talent, and that unless our industry, if called on, can measure up to that task, it cannot measure up to much else."

★ VI ★

Applying the Art of Persuasion

AMONG America's emissaries assigned to Foreign Service in the current Cold War is a diminutive cartoon character. He is known simply as Little Moe.

Few Americans know Little Moe, or have even heard of him. Yet our government's propaganda unit, the USIA, says that "Little Moe; His Life Behind the Iron Curtain" is the world's most widely read cartoon strip.

Little Moe, distributed overseas by USIA, is reportedly carried to from 50 to 75 million readers of some 1,200 newsapers in 50 foreign countries.

Of course, Little Moe has a job to do. Besides tickling funnybones, he is charged with carrying a message from the U. S. to readers the world over.

The message, broadly, is this: Life behind the Iron Curtain is not the "worker's paradise" that Red propagandists would have you believe.

And how does Little Moe go about this important task? He does it by depicting the Russian bully as inept, stupid, vain and easily outwitted! In strip after strip, Little Moe outfoxes or dupes his Red oppressor much as Mutt used to confound Jeff, or as Sad Sack (the World War II comic strip character after which Little Moe is modeled) outwitted his oafish sergeant.

Look at samples of the Little Moe strip and judge for yourself its persuasive power. To me it seems that by depicting the Communists in power as inept clowns, our government information agency is conveying messages that at best are of no value in the propaganda war, and at worst may be serving the enemy's purpose. The Soviets may be very pleased to be depicted as fools, undeserving of careful scrutiny and cautious relationships, like an affable con man who wants his victim to think him harmless. What better way to help still the alarm of those uncommitted nations that are wary lest Soviet aid put them in bondage to Communism, or those nations that think they can get twice as much aid by playing up to both sides? In the past the Russians have been most conciliatory at international conferences just before closing an iron fist around a startled, helpless nation.

Not long ago the UN and the world saw a clownish Khrushchev pound his shoe on the table in a seeming bit of boorish petulance, while at the same time a boisterous Castro was whooping it up in a New York hotel. Don't our information experts realize that such politically experienced men have an ulterior motive for such behavior; that they know how to gain an advantage by putting their opponents off guard by playing the role of stupid clowns? Little Moe may unwittingly be aiding the enemy by

LITTLE MOE: His Life Behind the Iron Curtain   by RIDEO

LITTLE MOE: His Life Behind the Iron Curtain   by RIDEO

LITTLE MOE: His Life Behind the Iron Curtain   by RIDEO

LITTLE MOE: His Life Behind the Iron Curtain   by RIDEO

making the Communist threat seem a fiction, an absurdity and a good laugh.

Despite its wide distribution and great potential and the importance the USIA seems to attach to it, Little Moe's content is determined almost entirely by one man, the chief of the Graphics Section of USIA and a former newspaper and magazine artist. He is guided primarily by "policy guidelines" sent intermittently to all USIA staff members from top echelon policymakers. He is given wide latitude in deciding how to ridicule the Communists.

Ridicule can, of course, be a most potent propaganda weapon, but when it produces a grossly distorted picture, the whole attempt may boomerang.

Little Moe is a glaring example of the importance that the USIA attaches to mere circulation and quantity, with insufficient regard for the much more vital ingredient of quality—the kind of material that will actually influence people's thinking and actions.

USIA seems mainly concerned with the "reach" of its messages—how many people listen to the Voice of America, how many newspapers carry its features, how many booklets it prints, how many people visit its centers. There is little evidence, in terms of results, to justify the quality of USIA's output. To be effective, any campaign must have a clear, well-defined objective, and the material distributed must contain words and pictures aimed at accomplishing it. But USIA tends to concentrate on projects that look impressive in statistical summaries. A veteran news correspondent in Latin America asserts that the USIA relies too heavily on the written word in areas where many if not most of the people are illiterate—the reason being that the

local USIA man who can place considerable copy in local
newspapers has something concrete to show his superiors
as evidence of his labors; and they in turn can use the
sheaf of clippings to good advantage when Congressional
committees want specific examples of what the agency is
doing. The fact that alternative activities might yield more
valuable, if less immediately tangible, results is often dis-
regarded.

Despite the lack of tangible achievements in the USIA
program, the Agency remains unconvinced that an advertising approach to its work would be an improvement on
its present policy.

An associate of mine once asked a USIA official why
they didn't use more advertising people to help with their
job of persuading the world to "buy" our "product." He
replied with a story about admen who were consulted by
another government agency during the early days of the
Marshall Plan. The task was to create interest in greater
productivity in France.

"One idea the advertising men came up with was to put
big neon signs on the Eiffel Tower," the USIA man said.
"The other idea was to manufacture a million yo-yo's with
slogans on the sides, and then send people around to hang
them on the bicycles of Frenchmen who were at work in
factories."

Now the geniuses who came up with these ideas may
indeed have been admen, though more probably they were
schooled in the field of Hollywood press agentry. But
their suggestions weren't *advertising*. Granted that advertisers often use signs and slogans, but they are most
often a part of a larger program using other media; they

are reminders which *enforce* the more traditional selling messages. But no matter what the medium, advertising agencies regularly conduct advance research to try to determine if the campaign is likely to accomplish its objective. And I think the most casual research would have shown a somewhat violent reaction to HELP THE MARSHALL PLAN emblazoned on the Eiffel Tower. Research would also have revealed what the USIA man already knew: Frenchmen don't know what a yo-yo is, or what to do with it, and indeed would probably have jailed anyone who rummaged about their bikes.

Such gimmicks would have been no more effective than many of the government's present efforts to sell our ideas abroad. But evidently they were the USIA official's idea of what admen would do if permitted to participate in our propaganda program. His view is indicative of the prejudice against and lack of understanding of the vocabulary of selling and advertising. When advertising efforts are bad—and some of them are—they can be ludicrous; but even when they are successful, they arouse criticism. People object to the idea that someone else is making up their minds for them. Many intellectuals complain that advertising has made our society so materialistic that it has turned away from aesthetic and spiritual values. But they do not note that Western civilization—brought to its present bountiful age in large measure through the development of commerce (of which advertising is an integral part)—has given rise to brilliantly conceived democracies, conquered many diseases, built universities, and given greater emphasis to individual human dignity than any other society in history.

It might be thought that the merits of our political and economic system are self-evident, that it is unnecessary to sell people something they already want and need. But this is not the case at all.

Consider the sewing machine invented by Elias Howe. This was an answer to the need and desire of women to make sewing an easier job. But what the history books overlook is that he couldn't get anyone to buy it. He was ahead of his time, not with his invention, but because modern promotion methods and merchandising techniques were not understood. He didn't know how to explain the sewing machine to prospective buyers—there was no concept of advertising to tell of the machine's benefits to consumers. It was accorded very little attention in this country for years. Although Howe was granted a patent for his machine in 1846, for a whole generation after that, women didn't even know it existed.

The telephone is another example of the classic truth in advertising—that a product rarely can be sold only on its self-evident merit. The telephone had to be sold before it became useful. While Alexander Graham Bell perfected his first telephone in 1875, commercial development was slow because potential users didn't know about or understand the telephone. Even by 1907, only 5 percent of the population of the United States were telephone subscribers.

By the same token, freedom and democracy will not be bought on their self-evident merits unless we effectively bring them to the attention of the people whom we want to influence. We cannot assume that the inhabitants of undeveloped nations, newly independent ones, or countries where there is widespread illiteracy will understand the merits of democracy without effort on our part. Moreover, our very survival may depend on our ability to overcome an unscrupulous competitor.

Obviously the Communists do not rely on the merits of Communism to sell their product. They use lies and half-truths with a complete lack of ethics. I am not suggesting that we counter lies with lies, or misrepresent what our way of life can offer to the rest of the world; I suggest rather that we adopt a persuasive program of truth which would—at the very least—offset the Communists' unscrupulous exploitation of the techniques of manipulating men's minds.

Robert Kennedy made note of the Communist techniques when reporting on his 1962 trip abroad. Often when a representative of the U. S. arrives in a country to explain the American point of view, "a small minority causes a riot, disturbs the performance or disrupts the speech," he said. "The incident makes headlines across the world and creates exactly the impression the Communists wish to create—that students oppose Americans. . . . We are victims of a smart, articulate, well-organized minority which has kept us continuously on the defensive. We have permitted it to happen; we have allowed it to continue. If we do not meet the problem head on, if we are not ourselves imaginative, tough, dedicated, willing and self-sacrificing, the struggle with the enemy will not be won by them, but lost by us.

"We have made mistakes, we have faults," he added. "We can admit them, tell of our progress, and talk of our accomplishments, material and spiritual. We have the truth on our side. But this is not enough. We must sell the truth."

Unfortunately, while Mr. Kennedy's perception of the problem is acute, his techniques for selling the truth seem very outmoded in this day of mass communications. His proposals include sending "groups of men and women to lecture, not just about the United States, and our form of government or about democracy generally, but also about history and philosophy and literature and even more practical matters. . . .

"Outside the auspices of government, I would also like to see private citizens, such as some of our university professors, playwrights and poets, as well as articulate businessmen and labor leaders, travel under the same kind of program. . . .

"I would have our government information agencies and services talk to other peoples more about fundamentals in the United States. I would have them explain the social progress being made in this country, what people are doing for one another, what contributions altruistic organizations such as the United Funds, March of Dimes and the Ford, Carnegie and Rockefeller foundations are making to the American way of life."

He also advocated that we "get people from our private sectors—from our artists, our poets, our musicians, our writers—to go into these countries and give lectures on areas in which they are experts, and stand up there and answer questions and meet with smaller groups of students at later dates and answer their questions and have exchanges. . . ."

I will not argue with any of these proposals, but they fall

far short of a complete campaign. What happened to the Robert Kennedy of two short years previous? In 1960, as his brother's campaign manager, he engineered a brilliant campaign to elect John F. Kennedy to the White House. Then, too, he faced the task of making an "unknown product" widely known. Did he rely solely on lectures and face-to-face meetings? Of course not. A careful campaign was mapped out, with the help of an advertising agency. Appeals for votes were made not on the basis of how good John Kennedy was, but on what he would do for the voters and the country if elected.

Mass media were employed extensively, not only in the televised debates, but for straightforward advertising messages.

Has Robert Kennedy now renounced such tactics as something less than nice—though expedient? I think not. I think he is merely afflicted with the same type of myopia which abounds in Washington, and around the country, for that matter. Advertising is considered all right for selling products, or for helping to elect candidates—even for such things as promoting public safety and fund-raising. But not for selling ideas to other nations.

The Peace Corps has been hailed as a great public relations weapon, showing the world how our idealistic young men and women will give up the comforts of this life to share their strength and knowledge with others less fortunate. This is certainly a commendable endeavor, but I wonder how effective it is as a weapon of propaganda.

In early 1964 the Peace Corps had about 8,000 volunteers serving in 46 countries. Many of them are serving in remote areas and come in contact with only a handful of people.

Against this is the incessant Red propaganda operating in these countries, tagging the volunteers as imperialist spies, agents of the Central Intelligence Agency. The charge that Peace Corps Volunteers are in fact CIA agents is a constant one, obviously the line the Kremlin has selected to counteract the Corps.

"The people just laugh at those spy charges," say the volunteers returning to the U. S. And to those who come in direct contact with these fine young men and women, the charge probably does seem silly.

But there are millions and millions of people in these countries. Only a few know the Peace Corps from first-hand experience. How about all the others? Do they believe this constant Red propaganda? Do they laugh at the charges? Perhaps, at first. But do they laugh when these charges are repeated, day after day, with no counter-effort on our part?

The Peace Corps, on its own, is a praiseworthy—but minuscule—effort to win the minds of men. Without an effective campaign of propaganda aimed at the masses of people in these countries, the Peace Corps is a new target for the Big Red Lie.

The Red machine is ready to seize on any misstep. A postcard from volunteer Margery Michelmore went astray in Nigeria, and turned up in the hands of Communist sympathizers. It described the "squalor and primitiveness" of the country, and the publicity this caused far outweighed the patient labors of Miss Michelmore and the other volunteers.

Certainly the people-to-people programs are useful for supplementing our total selling effort, but they do not take the place of a skillful, professionally planned campaign. Personal selling is often very effective, but it is also the most costly and the slowest means of selling. Personal selling also has the drawback of personal bias. Persuasion is most powerful when it is based on a clear, concise message that is repeated again and again. By asking many persons untutored in the techniques of advertising to convey our complex story abroad, we invite inconsistent interpretations of fact which may cause confusion and destroy their effectiveness. By all means we should encourage our best artists, writers, musicians and scholars to represent us abroad, and we should maintain our Peace Corps; but we should remember that approaches to people on the aesthetic and cultural level reach only a tiny percentage of the population of any country; and that the sincerest efforts of Peace Corps members will not triumph over all the obstacles that Soviet propaganda puts in their way. Our artists may be well versed in their own art, and can do a good job of presenting our cultural achievements. But how will they react in situations when they are confronted by trained Communist propagandists, when trained agitators stop a performance or interrupt a speech? Even such politically astute men as Robert Kennedy and Richard Nixon admit having trouble when such incidents occur.

Some private organizations play a useful role in carrying our messages abroad. Radio Free Europe, based in Munich, and Radio Liberty, both privately supported networks, broadcast effectively in their target areas—but these areas are limited largely to countries behind the Iron

Curtain, and the networks' resources are limited. If our current psychological war *is* war, then these networks are something like an army supported by a fund-raising drive.

The Cold War Council in Los Angeles is a private organization whose function is to press for a greater propaganda effort, but it does not actually propagandize.

The Advertising Council today expends nearly half its efforts on behalf of the U. S. Government. During World War II it mustered the forces of advertising in a national emergency and has been working for government projects ever since. In addition to promoting Smokey Bear for the Conservation Department and U. S. Savings Bonds for the Treasury Department, the Peace Corps and a four-part campaign on the Promise of America, it also works for such public service organizations as the Red Cross, National Safety Council and American Cancer Society, and such causes as mental health, employment for the physically handicapped and religion in American life, to name but a few. The Advertising Council's job is to sell ideas and a few products—like U. S. Savings Bonds—to Americans in America, not to conduct an overseas propaganda program.

Another organization, the Adequate U. S. Overseas Information Program, is working for the objective stated in its name. This group is working for more enlightened use of propaganda. Its function is not to propagandize.

The fact remains, the responsibility for propaganda rests solely with the United States Government. Only our government has the power to call up sufficient resources and manpower to wage a massive propaganda war effectively and continuously. Only a government agency, working closely with the President and top administration officials, can effectively mount a propaganda drive which will be harmonious with government policy.

In view of our half-measures and our failure to use effective means of propaganda, the concept of advertising in this context begins to make sense. We lead the world in our ability to create desire for advertised products. This has not come about merely by chance. It has happened because advertising men know how to make advertising do its job: to get definite, measurable results. Successful advertising is persuasion, and successful persuasion motivates action. This does not apply only to products; it applies also to the acceptance of ideas.

We balk at the idea of using persuasion to put across the ideas of freedom and democracy, though we all use persuasion in our daily lives. An able lawyer can persuade a jury on behalf of his clients; in fact, he is expected to do so. The gifted educator, the one whose classes are jammed, is surely a persuasive individual. A physician builds a successful practice not solely because he is competent but because he convinces (persuades) his patients that he will do everything in his power to cure them. Even children understand persuasion. Watch how, once they stumble onto the power of a smile, they use it to persuade us.

Each of these persons uses persuasion to achieve results, and all these kinds of persuasion are effective. They may not spring from a conscious effort; they can be spontaneous, but they are nonetheless intentional, willed efforts to make ourselves acceptable, to establish our relationships with other people, to find the grounds of mutual agreement.

Some children and some adults never learn the power of a smile. Some lawyers have no courtroom presence or forensic skill, and must remain the scholars and interpreters of law. Some educators, however brilliant, cannot communicate their ideas when they face a large class in a lecture hall, and must convey their knowledge through seminars or by writing books. But everyone who has a talent, knowledge, or idea—or a product of use or value to others—must have a way of articulating what he has to offer.

Advertising deliberately uses the art of persuasion in all its refinements and subtleties, and with a polished, professional skill. It uses it consciously and with purpose, and is often able to measure the result. Good advertising is used scrupulously, it is based on confidence in what it sells, and it presents the product (or idea or image) it is selling in its best light. It is unnecessary, in fact it is harmful, to make false claims for a good product or idea; but it is necessary to make it known.

The art of persuasion involves five distinct steps. First of all, *attention* must be gained by the persuading agent. Then, *interest* must be created. Next, *desire* must be aroused and *action* must be stimulated. When these elements are translated to words or pictures they must be *communicated repeatedly*, day after day, to the greatest number of people of the group to be persuaded, until the idea is finally accepted. Advertising deliberately seeks ways to combine these elements; when it does not do so it fails.

Repetition has a built-in fatigue factor for some people. Nevertheless it is necessary in selling an idea. It is part of human nature to accept as fact what one hears repeatedly. The Communists have used this psychological phenomenon to their great advantage; they have repeated their claims over and over, until their misrepresentations have become "truth" in the minds of many. We consider the truths of freedom and democracy to be self-evident because we have been exposed to these facts from our earliest years. But in reaching people who do not know them, we must drive across our point continuously. And we must find ways of reaching and holding the attention of those whom we wish to persuade.

VII

The *"Madison Avenue" Myth*

ATTACKS on advertising by authors and scholars have helped to direct a barrage of abuse at the advertising profession. In educational and cultural circles it is felt that our age is too fast, too shallow, too materialistic; and somehow much of the blame is placed on the glib admen.

Today, the Gray Flannel Suit Boys, the Hidden Persuaders, Madison Avenue, are popular scapegoats for Americans upset by an ever-quickening tempo of life and an ever-increasing din of printed and electronic communications.

As *Time* magazine said, "Debate about advertising is not new to the U. S. At one time or another, virtually every American of consequence has passed judgment on the industry."

Much of this "judgment" has been unfavorably critical. Some of this adverse criticism is valid; much of it is not.

Ted Repplier, president of the Advertising Council, in

a talk at a luncheon of the leaders for Education in New York City, urged the educators:

> Please understand me. I am not suggesting that educators cease criticizing advertising, but merely that they be 1) fair and 2) specific. Neither am I defending all advertising, although perhaps 95 percent of the advertising which finds its way into print in magazines and newspapers offends no one. Ninety-five percent, by the way, is not perfect but it is not bad. Some might question whether the actions of less publicized professions—like law and medicine—would score any higher. However, I should be the first to admit that far too many of the commercials currently on television are stupid, or exaggerated or in frightful taste. But for heaven's sake, when criticizing advertising may we not have some of that fine objectivity for which educators are famous?

If I am to suggest that our government should use advertising executives in the fight against the encroachment of Communism, then it follows that I should explain these attacks on advertising, and why these attacks do not render invalid the claim that advertising executives represent a tremendous pool of vital talent for our government.

The advertising business has its fair share of people who have little—or dubious—taste. There are people in advertising who have no imagination. There are people who stoop to gimmickry and tricks to attract attention. For the most part these gimmicks and tricks do not add to the effectiveness of the advertising. More often they interfere. They are used on the theory—one which I do not subscribe to—that just because the advertising attracts attention it will sell merchandise. It takes more than consumer awareness of a product or a company to produce results.

The use of raucous, unpleasant attention-getting devices doesn't please me any more than it does the critics of advertising. I resent them as much as anyone else—perhaps more, because I know that advertising should be tasteful and imaginative. And much of the *effective* advertising is in good taste.

One of my favorite definitions of advertising and its function is that of Fairfax M. Cone, chairman of the executive committee of Foote, Cone & Belding. Mr. Cone, in addition to heading one of the ten largest advertising agencies in the country, is a leading spokesman for his profession and an active civic and community leader.

Mr. Cone says this simple sentence sums up his whole philosophy: "Advertising is something you do when you can't go see somebody."

Mr. Cone feels advertising "should be as close to what you would say to me, if you came to see me about a business proposition, as you could put into print or onto film. And if you make it as much like you would be coming to see me, then it's going to be honest, straightforward and tasteful—all the good things. Advertising gets bad when people forget this and they try to make it into something else."

When some critics are offended in some manner by an ad, or a certain kind of advertising campaign, they attack the entire profession of advertising.

Would these people be critical of the advertising campaigns that have reaped enormous sums of money for worthy charities? Would they criticize the role of the advertising profession in promoting fire safety in our national parks, forests and game preserves?

Would they criticize the highly successful efforts of the advertising profession in selling war bonds in a time of national peril?

Would they criticize advertising for providing the tremendous, constant flow of information about many new products and the improvements in known products?

Do they object to the retail food advertising that gives their families the information about when and where they may buy the necessities of daily living at the best price? Do they object to the constant flow of information about quality and value described in retail department store advertising?

I wonder; do these critics object to the advertising that informs people about educational institutions—where they are and what they have to offer to the young men and women of America?

Do they object to the fact that advertising makes it possible for this country to have a free press? It does; if there were no advertising, then publishers would have to be subsidized by the government or some special-interest groups. Circulation alone cannot and does not support any large-scale venture in newspaper or periodical publishing.

Do the critics object to the widest variety of entertainment in the world provided free of charge on radio and television by paid advertising? Maybe they don't like what is presented, but can they offer a substitute to the mass of people, including the aged, ill and lonely, who look to radio and television as their major form of companionship, relaxation and entertainment?

Do they object to paid advertising making possible, free, the news and public service broadcasts that bring the events of the world into their living rooms, helping to make Americans the best informed people on earth?

Do they object to the broadcasts that bring our public officials to the microphone and camera to report on what they are doing, so that the public can make better judgments at the polls? Advertising revenues permit stations to devote free time to civic purposes at no cost to the taxpayer.

I do not think they object to any of these things. I am sure that most of those who criticize advertising in general do not stop to think that advertising does have these additional useful purposes.

As *Time* magazine in its article "The Visible Persuaders" pointed out, although today Americans talk about advertising more than ever because it has "woven itself inextricably into the texture of their everyday lives," they don't understand the advertising business. Because of movies like *The Hucksters* (based on a novel of the same name) and *Lover Come Back,* in the public mind "the advertising business is firmly established as a gray-flannel world of three-Gibson lunches, three-button jackets, unabashed throat slicing and zany argot."

What people should object to—and here I am wholeheartedly with them—is bad advertising. Antagonism is justified when advertising resorts to unpleasant gimmicks and noise to sell a product. When advertising is geared to a basic human need and the useful purposes of a product are described, that in itself is enough to gain the attention and interest of the reader or listener, and at the same time do a better advertising job.

Not all the people in the business of advertising are

ethical and/or knowledgeable. Merely to admit that some of the practitioners of advertising are tasteless boors—or worse—does not answer all the complaints. There still remain complaints about advertising that is tasteful, knowledgeable and informative.

Perhaps some of this criticism stems from the unavoidable fact that someone is "selling" something to somebody. Apparently the elements involved in selling, the act of selling itself, seems to have a negative psychological effect on some people. This is, admittedly, perhaps a shallow hypothesis. Yet, the 1960 edition of Webster's *New World Dictionary of the American Language* does list, in the definition of the word *sell*, the following alternate meanings:

> ... to give up or deliver (a person) to his enemies or into slavery, bondage, etc. ... to betray (a country, cause, etc.); to give up (one's honor, trust, etc.) for profit.

Maybe this is the reason that you often hear a salesman say, "I'm not trying to sell you anything, but ..." Certainly he is trying to sell something but he seems to feel that there is some automatic opposition to his being a salesman. People, when they know they are being sold, often resent it. They like to feel that they can decide on the merits of a product or idea themselves, rather than take as gospel what someone else might say about it. Naturally people want to make their own choices, even though their decisions are frequently influenced by outside factors.

It is part of the advertising man's job to understand these outside factors, to use them in selling his client's product, and to satisfy the purchaser that the product is what he wanted. Surveys have clearly shown that people on all educational and economic levels respond to advertising, and that consciously or subconsciously, they ascribe the same qualities to the product as the advertiser does, sometimes without being aware that they have seen or heard the ads. In this case they have certainly been influenced by an "outside" factor.

For example, a group of women who were interviewed (in a study by Psychological Corporation) to determine why they bought a certain product gave reasons that would indicate they were motivated by their own judgment. They rarely mentioned advertising as the stimulus. Yet the phrases they used in describing the product were the same as those used in the advertising. Product surveys invariably show this to be true.

For instance, if a certain beer is advertised as having a "smooth" taste, persons who drink that brand will say they do because they like its smoothness. Likewise car buyers often use the well-known advertising slogans when telling why they selected their particular make of car. There are several reasons for this. An advertising man knows that one of his tasks is to give regular consumers of a product a continuing feeling of satisfaction with their purchase. Another reason may be that the advertising copywriter has accurately described the qualities of a product, so that consumers say a beer is "smooth" because in fact it is. Persuasion can mean simply an honest presentation of the facts—information of interest and value to the person to whom it is offered.

But the connotations that have grown up around such words as "propaganda," "sell," "advertising" and "persuasion" have clouded their true meanings and their real uses and value.

Results of an exhaustive survey of opinions of college men about selling, and their grasp of its function, caused Sylvia Porter, syndicated newspaper financial columnist, to comment:

> The great productive machinery of the United States can turn out hundreds of billions of dollars of goods each year. But unless the goods are marketed, advertised, sold with boldness, faith and pride, they'll back up in warehouses, businesses will go bankrupt, jobs will disappear and our whole economy will falter.
>
> Crucial to our nation's prosperity are the attitudes we have toward those who sell what industry produces, the incentives we give to salesmen and our understanding of the vital role that selling plays in a consumer's economy.
>
> These points are obvious to every thoughtful observer of America's economy today. Thus the findings of an exhaustive survey of the opinions held by college men about selling and of their grasp of selling's function are shocking.
>
> Only one male college student in 17 is willing to try selling as a career.
>
> Three-fourths of male students consider selling at best only a job, at worst a racket.
>
> Of the 69 percent of today's college males who already have decided on their careers, only 5 percent have chosen sales.
>
> The biggest student objection to sales work is that it is "forcing people to buy things they don't need."
>
> An oft-repeated comment is: "If people want things they know where to get them; selling fills no economic need." This remark reflects an abominable lack of understanding of what selling is all about.
>
> From a Yale student came this: "It's both too frus-

trating and too prostituting." (That word came up frequently.) From an Oregon State youngster trying to be open-minded came the statement that he wouldn't mind selling a product of "profound significance to the consumer," but he had never found such a product.

The negative impression about the job security of salesmen is just as bad. The beliefs are that if anything goes wrong, salesmen are the first to be fired and that salesmen exist only on commissions and have no guaranteed income.

"It's cockeyed," says Sales Management, "but the important point is that the students do feel this way."

If we were still in the first post-World War II years, when demands for goods were so powerful that all the emphasis was on production and salesmen had only to be order-takers, these attitudes would be disturbing but not dangerous.

But today we can produce far more than we are selling. Today, we are competing against aggressive manufacturers and marketing men the world over. Successful distribution of the goods we turn out—and at the heart of this is aggressive selling—has become of crucial importance to our prosperity.

But businessmen and teachers can and should grab this challenge on their own. In view of today's economic world, it's imperative that all of us re-examine our attitudes toward the men and women who move the goods that America produces.*

Advertising is, of course, a vital and necessary part of selling and it seems to share the same stigma. But if people understand the functions of advertising and if the advertising is persuasive and in good taste, their objections to it can be overcome.

* Used by permission of The Hall Syndicate, Inc.

In the years I have headed an advertising agency, I have come across many instances of misunderstandings of the meanings and uses of the words "advertising" and "selling." After a little clarification, followed by results, these misunderstandings were always cleared up.

A number of years ago one of the trustees of the Girls' Latin School in Chicago, anxious to help get students when enrollment was lagging, suggested to the head of the school that an advertising man be called in. When the headmistress was first approached, she looked aghast and said, "Of course we don't want any advertising or promotional material."

She didn't think much of the idea of using an adman to help solve the school's problems, but reluctantly agreed to call us in for a trial.

After we researched the problem to find out why more students were not seeking to enroll at the school, we decided to use a letter directed to parents of prospective students. The letters were produced and presented to the head of the school. She was most enthusiastic about the letters because they did not contain what she considered the usual advertising vocabulary. She felt that they merely put forth in an extremely effective way the reasons why girls could benefit by attending the school. Incidentally, the letters brought results and the enrollment quota was filled.

Early in World War II, I went to Washington to consult with U. S. Navy public relations executives on behalf of one of our clients, with the idea of selling our Navy to the American public at a time when it was being severely criticized. Commander Jack Hartley, head of public relations, said, "Good grief, we don't want to sell the Navy—we want to keep it."

After consultation with our client, a subsequent meeting was arranged, and this time we carefully avoided using the vocabulary of the advertising business. It was suggested to Commander Hartley that we tell some of the great traditions of the U. S. Navy and how effectively the Navy was meeting current problems. The idea was accepted with enthusiasm. Because of the generosity of our client, our agency worked with the Navy for the remainder of the war. As a matter of fact, we reached the point where the Navy would simply give us their public relations problems and let us solve them as we saw best. But this came to pass only when the misunderstandings about advertising and advertising techniques were cleared up and they gained confidence in our ability.

Arthur J. Schlesinger Jr., professor at Harvard University, and often a top adviser to government leaders, frequently expresses his hostility toward advertising men, ignoring the many contributions that they have made to the economy.

He depicts advertising, along with advertising men, as a force that is working against the public welfare. He has quoted John Ruskin as follows:

> Whatever happens to you, this, at least, is certain, that the whole of your life will have been spent in corrupting public taste and encouraging public extravagance. Every preference you have won by gaudiness must have been based on the purchaser's vanity; every demand you have created by novelty has fostered in the consumer a habit of discontent. . . .

It is apparently his point of view that people are "foolish enough to buy products just because they are advertised."

Of course, this is not so. In our own time we have the classic example of the Edsel, a Ford Motor Company auto which cost $250,000,000 to bring to market, including an expenditure of more than $12,000,000 for introductory advertising. Despite this, the car lasted on the market for only about three years. The public cannot be sold a product they don't want, regardless of how much it is advertised.

Harvard University, which has supplied a good many of our government advisers, has more than its share of critics who attack advertising on something less than a rational basis. Professor Alvin Hansen, in his book *Economic Issues of the 1960's,* suggests that we "get rid of the decadent influence of advertising."

In a talk given as the Radcliffe baccalaureate address, Professor Raphael Demos, Harvard University philosopher, said:

> As you go out into the larger world, you will not find it easy to be reasonable when surrounded by the waves of passion and subjected to the dark and subtle pressures of the society in which you will live. You will be assailed by spell-binders and tempted by the magnetic voices of the demagogues and the fanatics. You may be unprepared for this encounter just because you have been protected while in college from such onslaughts. . . . I mean advertising. More and more, advertisers aim to manipulate us, to put our reason to sleep, and to awaken instead our unconscious motivations. In addition, they seem to say— and say falsely—that material possessions, comforts, luxuries, add up to the good life. . . .

I think that this is an insult to the intelligence of today's college graduates and their ability to make good judgments and form their own opinions about what they do or don't want.

The late Bernard De Voto, Harvard professor, and the author of many books, castigates advertising as a "cult, a system of magic, practiced by magicians, witch doctors, sorcerers and shamans...."

These are cruel attacks on all advertising men and are not presented with the objectivity that scholars and educators should have.

You cannot describe advertising or advertising people with one term any more than you can describe education and educators with one term. Advertising is practiced by people with as many different types of skills and personal characteristics as exist in human life.

Time magazine editors recognized this when they said in their article on advertising:

> To do the job that otherwise would require millions of salesmen, the U. S. has spawned more than 500 advertising agencies of some size and stature. The backbone of the business consists of the 42 major agencies that have billings of more than $25 million a year.
> ... Contrary to legend, the top U. S. agencies are just as diverse in character and outlook as 42 individual salesmen would be....

Good advertising is nothing more than *the presentation of information through mass media, emphasizing the benefits of what is offered*. The art of persuasion, properly used, does not necessarily involve high pressure. As a matter of fact, people often resent pressure and will turn away from the product so offered.

Another factor that arouses criticism of advertising is the interruption of entertainment programs for commercials. More and more advertising now is coming to people through the medium of free entertainment—television.

An alternative would be government radio and television, the cost of which would be borne by set owners through taxes, with standards of entertainment likely to be far below what we have now. Several countries which have experimented with government television, notably England and Canada, are moving rapidly in the direction of the advertising-supported system used in the United States.

Another factor that causes some people to dislike advertising is the necessary element of repetition.

You cannot say only once that untended fires and carelessness with matches, cigarettes, cigars and pipes are menaces to our national forests. You must say it over and over again. The knack is to do it in as nice a way as possible. While this is not always easy, it is being accomplished in a vast number of advertising messages daily.

In other cases, effective repetition is accomplished by the use of straight, commonsense words describing the product; at other times by entertainment devices, good illustrations, pleasant music or use of personalities.

Part of the problem is that there is a difference in the irritation quotient of different economic and cultural groups. Some people—usually at the high end of the educational and economic scale—seem to dislike the commercial interruptions on television more than the general

viewer. The mass of people look upon advertising as help-
ful information about certain products; some people actually look forward to the commercials with interest.

Most advertising is aimed at the biggest-spending market. That market happens to be the people who earn $150
a week or less. Most products and services available in
our economy are purchased by this huge economic bloc.
It follows that most consumer advertising is aimed at this
market. This causes some objections from those who find
the "median level appeal" annoying.

When an advertising medium is directed to one group
or class, there rarely is a problem. Some television and
radio stations, magazines and other publications gear their
material to specialized groups. The advertising copy then
is directed to that group on their own educational or cultural level. But as long as those in the upper economic
and cultural groups, representing a minority, listen to or
read the media that appeal to the mass, there is bound to
be some antagonism.

It is not unusual for people in the higher educational
groups to assume that the language they use is understood
by everyone. There is only one sure way of communicating
with the great mass of people through mass media, and
that is with the simplest possible words. To do this, an
advertiser may have to "abuse the intelligence" of the
group with a higher education level.

I believe that in general all mass media are making an
effort to upgrade their audience or readers, but this must
of necessity be a gradual development; otherwise these
media would lose their following.

The American Association of Advertising Agencies, the

National Association of Broadcasters, the Association of National Advertisers, the Better Business Bureau, the Federal Trade Commission, the Federal Communications Commission, many radio and television stations and other groups are constantly working to improve the standards of advertising. The vast majority of advertising professionals are working hard to discourage bad advertising.

Certainly, some advertising has its puffery, but to a large degree this is self-defeating to the life of the product, for no consumer will continue to buy a product that has not lived up to its claims. In addition, many consumers buy products from retailers with whom they trade regularly and who will refund the purchaser's money if the product is not satisfactory. Further, advertising actually can do more harm than good for a bad product by constantly reminding a dissatisfied user of claims the product cannot meet. Some of the early home permanent products, for example, quietly vanished from the market because they didn't work. Heavy promotion behind their introduction served to irritate the consumers who had tried them.

While I do not condone puffery in advertising, it is used in almost every profession, particularly by some politicians running for public office. Isn't it puffery when the politician criticizes his opponents and then makes promises to the voters that he cannot fulfill; or when he expresses ideas in speeches that are prepared by professional writers, misleading the public in representing these ideas as his own?

To be perfectly honest, a political candidate should, when he makes a speech, state that the speech was prepared with the cooperation of writers and advisers, lest the public interpret the speech as being entirely his own.

Political spokesmen often criticize advertising; seldom are they willing to be specific.

Once in a while these critics uncover a Tartar. Three rather important political spokesmen discovered this when they delivered to a national audience a clutch of disparaging remarks about "Madison Avenue" during the 1960 political conventions.

Leo Burnett, head of the advertising agency that bears his name, answered these critics in a paid advertisement in the *Wall Street Journal:*

> Like most critics of advertising you stuck to innuendo and avoided specifics.
>
> As a matter of fact, you all sounded suspiciously like people in need of a little more information on the subject.
>
> We think you might feel differently about advertising if you knew more about it. Accordingly, we invite you to spend a week at our agency as our guests. We'll pay all your expenses. We'll hide nothing from you.
>
> We urge you to sit with our management in Creative Review Group meetings where we evaluate campaigns, to visit with our research, marketing and creative people, or anyone else in the agency with whom you'd like to talk.
>
> When you have done this, ask yourself these questions:
>
> 1. Do these people work hard and conscientiously to tell consumers the truth about the products they advertise?
>
> 2. How do the ethics, intelligence, and practices of advertising people compare with those of the people entrusted with the conduct of our state and national governments?

> After that, you might like to apologize to the advertising business.

Nobody accepted the invitation, and none of the three men apologized.

When all the charges of "hidden persuaders" and "manipulators" are cleared away, advertising emerges simply as a tool of marketing.

The very best test of its acceptance, despite the small, peripheral area of criticism, is that advertising has been—and is—one of the tools responsible for our astoundingly high standard of living.

David Potter, professor of history at Yale, in his book *People of Plenty*, had this to say about advertising and its relationship to our abundant American society:

> Advertising as such is by no means a neglected subject. The excesses of advertising and of advertising men have been a favorite theme for a full quorum of modern satirists, cynics and Jeremiahs. . . . Since advertising lends itself both to aesthetic criticism and to moral criticism and since humanity is ever ready with views in each of these areas, the flow of opinion has been copious.
>
> But advertising as an institution has suffered almost total neglect. One might read fairly widely in the literature which treats of public opinion, popular culture and the mass media in the United States without ever learning that advertising now compares with such long-standing institutions as the school and the church in the magnitude of its social influence.

Professor Potter concludes his chapters on advertising with:

> Such a transformation in our economy, brought about by the need to stimulate desire for the goods which an

abundant economy has to offer and which a scarcity economy would never have produced, offers strong justifica-
tion for the view that advertising should be recognized as
an important social influence and as our newest major institution—an institution peculiarly identified with one of
the most pervasive forces in American life, the force of
economic abundance.

I believe that the critics of advertising, some of them
fair, sincere and thoughtful, but the majority unfair, un-
thinking, and not justified in their criticism, have had an
undue influence on government. This influence has had
its effect; the techniques and skills of advertising executives for the most part are conspicuously ignored by government.

In the profession of advertising there are thousands of
dedicated, highly creative, widely informed executives
who could be of inestimable value to their country. If
criticism of a small segment of their business is sufficient
to bar them from being of service to their government and
their fellow citizens, then indeed, this is the most unfair
indictment ever based on an uninformed minority opinion.

VIII

Agency X

Is it wrong to "sell" the story of the United States abroad? Not unless *all* selling is wrong.

Should we assume that all people have the intelligence to discover things which are right and good, without being pressured by someone else? Not unless we assume *all* persuasion is unnecessary.

In part, the policy of the U. S. Information Agency is to tell the world the truth of what is happening, in the belief that people will automatically feel favorable to us, particularly if they are given the unbiased news of what is happening in the world.

This policy is continued, although it has failed over and over again. We are losing the War of Words.

All too often we merely say to people of other nations, in effect, "Here is our great system of government; here is how we live. Why don't you do the same? How does Communism compare to us? We're just the best, that's all."

We spend a lot of money doing this and we have wasted

a great deal of time. The Communists spend more than we do—much more, in fact—but they have learned that the techniques used by American advertising are sound and they use them to tremendous advantage.

I have said that many advertising executives are particularly qualified to advise and direct the work of communications with a purpose. Let's take a look at this man in his most common environ, the advertising agency.

The first thing we will find is that, like many other characters of the "good old days," the all-purpose genius who prepared all phases of an advertising campaign has not been able to survive. Present competitive conditions require a group of specialists working together to produce a successful campaign.

Let's suppose that this group of specialists—this agency —is confronted with the task of introducing a new product. They have at their disposal all the tools of advertising. Now advertising is simply a type of visual or auditory communication designed to motivate people—to purchase a product, accept an idea or take some other action desired by the communicator. An advertising agency deals in this type of communication on behalf of its clients. When a problem in selling is presented, it is tackled as a purely business problem with a definite result to be obtained.

To motivate people through the use of words or pictures, those words or pictures must convey a benefit that is accepted, consciously or unconsciously.

For example, let's say our new product is a cold drink. Since the desire to drink something refreshing already exists, a good advertisement channels that desire toward a certain brand to fulfill that desire.

In order for any product or idea offered in an advertisement to be accepted, a basic need for it must already exist. This need may be a physiological or a psychological one; but unless it exists, the possibilities for the advertising to be successful are remote.

Psychologists have classified basic needs in different ways. Whether the need for survival covers them all is often debated, but it at least covers a wide range. Directly tied to survival are the needs for shelter, comfort and security. We can break these down even further into the need to satisfy hunger and thirst, the need for activity and for relaxation, the need for love, social approval, and self-esteem. One can perhaps add many more. But we all know that different people place different values on these basic needs—without, perhaps, recognizing their needs by these names. And some people value one need above all others.

The advertising man must discover what needs are connected with his product, and then center his communications around the satisfaction of these needs by his product. Therefore, the agency, in working out its campaign, must know everything possible about the product and its market.

In general, the agency wants to know what the product is made of, how it is manufactured, what are its special features, and what group of people are most likely to use the product. Then, the task is to learn everything possible about this group of likely prospects—age, income, occupation, etc. The agency also will want to know how long it will take to consume the product, what types of outlets are best suited for distribution of the product, what price it should sell for, what the regional problems are, and what competitive problems exist. Most—preferably all—of this information must be available before the job can proceed.

Let's take a closer look at our advertising agency. We'll call it Agency X. Our Agency X is not identical with all other agencies for the simple reason that agencies vary widely in their organizations and procedures. But it is typical.

At the very top level is the administrator, who is the organizer, and coordinates all departments of the advertising agency. The administrator appoints a project supervisor for each major client project. The project supervisor works with the Plans Group, which is composed of highly trained specialists from each department—creative, media, research and marketing.

The research specialist must know a vast amount about all the tools of research; what methods of research are pertinent to the problem faced, how to apply them, where to obtain specialists in particular types of research, and how to interpret and evaluate the research obtained.

The second specialist is the creative director. He is the highly creative, sensitive person who is skilled in preparing the means—the pictures and the words—of presenting the advertising message to the audience.

The media specialist is expert in determining what method should be used to present the message to the desired audience. He selects the vehicle, the medium to be used, and if there is no satisfactory medium available, he must try to develop one.

The marketing director, who works with the project supervisor, in addition to giving general guidance on sales

AGENCY X

Simplified Organization Chart of an Advertising Agency Operation

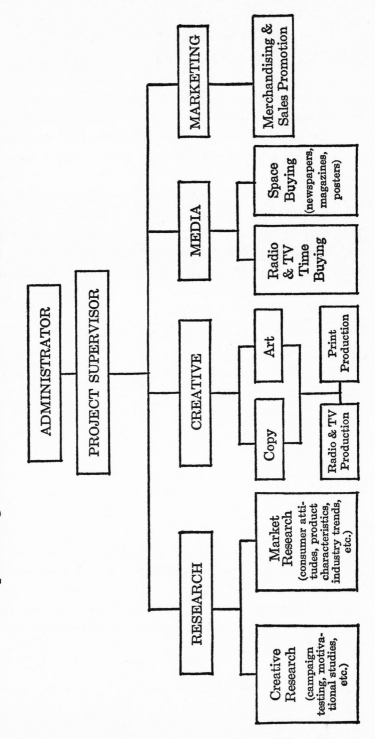

opportunities, has under his direction the merchandising of a campaign.

This, then, is our Plans Group. Besides being creative, they are all aware of the basic problems of selling. This group meets to examine the product and review the information that has been furnished to them by the manufacturer. At this meeting they will decide what general course the campaign will take, requesting from the research department what further information they need. At a second meeting, when the research is completed, they block out in some detail their views, which are then checked with the client. After approval, the material is distributed to the various departments, including copy, art, media and merchandising, for the final development of the campaign. The approved material is known as the Copy Platform.

The spotlight then moves to the copy man, the true creative force in the agency. It is his work, based on what research has told him, that the public will see or hear. He is the persuader, the one who must convince his audience that the product should be purchased, or the idea accepted.

The Copy Platform is the policy of the campaign and the copywriter must never lose sight of his main objective.

Copywriters that I have known—and I have known many—are nothing like the type indicated by the term "Madison Avenue." They are often sensitive, quiet, introverted people with a great deal of human understanding, with built-in antennae that seem to be constantly reaching out for an understanding of the underlying motives that make people do things.

When preparing advertising for a mass market item, the copywriter generally aims his message to the largest mass of people—and they come within the middle and lower income groups, as well as those with more limited education. Without their approval and financial support, a product for mass distribution cannot be a success. The copywriter therefore usually limits his copy to the simplest language in order to be certain that his message will be understood.

Given an unlimited vocabulary, and with no limitation on the number of words, anyone who can write can prepare an acceptable message about a product and its uses. But to write an effective advertising message that will be understood by the masses, with all the necessary appeals, and with the limitations of space and time, requires great copy skills. The words make the reader or viewer stop long enough to receive the sales message.

An important member of our team—the media director —is probably not well known outside the advertising field. But his task of selecting and providing the media is essential. It is not unusual for people not experienced in advertising to create an effective message but fail to provide the proper means for its most effective exposure.

The vehicle must reach the audience which is the prime sales target for your product. This sounds easy. If you want to reach women, advertise in women's magazines, or on daytime television; if your product is for men, advertise in men's magazines or on televised sports events. But sometimes the task is much more complicated. An insurance advertiser, for instance, may want to reach men, but not just any men. He wants men with above-average income, but not so old as to be poor insurance risks. Where to reach this youngish man with a rising income? Well, he's probably got a college education, so his TV viewing will probably include a good news documentary. The advertiser may reach fewer total number of people on the news show than if he sponsored a popular comedian, but he may reach far more *prospects* on the news show. The media department of his advertising agency should be able to answer this question for him.

This area of media investigation requires considerable research. Every possible avenue of approach to the audience to be reached must be explored. It may be that no ordinary or existing method will work properly. The media expert must be creative enough to supply a new means of communication to reach his audience.

Once the Agency X Plans Board has seen that the research is done, the Copy Platform decided upon and the method of reaching the audience determined, the actual mechanics of the advertising program go into gear.

At this point the marketing man brings into play his merchandising cooperation.

As a simple example, let us assume that you have seen an ad for a certain brand of hat. You've seen it many times in many different places. But you've more or less forgotten about it. Then one day you are shopping for a hat and you see that brand in a store. The display where the hat is shown is keyed to the advertisements that you have seen—and that you had apparently forgotten. But subconsciously you do remember those ads, and the store display triggers that remembrance in your mind. Thus the brand is not "strange" to you, and perhaps this factor will affect your decision on which brand of hat you eventually purchase.

An important function of merchandising specialists is to take advantage of the preconditioning and make the displays at the point of purchase "key in" to the prior advertising.

With the advertising messages now being delivered, another phase begins. A good advertising agency—and Agency X is a good agency—considers the launching of a carefully thought-out campaign only the beginning of the work. Almost immediately the agency group sets out to discover what is happening in the marketplace. They start almost anew and probe every area of the campaign to find out if it is operating as they planned it to operate.

Survey organizations are available to tell you what is happening at the point of sale—whether people are purchasing your product or not. But this information is normally not available for some time, and Agency X will want immediate information on how the audience is receiving the campaign.

If you get out into the field quickly and measure the degree to which the consumer is reacting to the ads, you will know that if he continues on this course he will or will not buy your product. This follow-up research may call for adjustments in the advertising campaign.

For the truth of the matter is that, despite the charges that advertising men are devious and unfailing manipulators of human behavior, no one can predict with certainty how people will react to a campaign. Pre-testing of ads on a small group, or, in some instances, a single market, helps, but it is not infallible. A campaign launched with high hopes and great confidence may founder very quickly, putting in jeopardy a large advertising fund.

And this is where the advertising agency shows its mettle. The ability to find out what is wrong, and correct it —fast—is the key to success. Maybe it isn't your advertising. Maybe your competitor just happened to begin giving away free samples that week; or perhaps the product needs to be redesigned to overcome some flaw. Whatever the reason, advertising agency researchers must be able to find the trouble. It takes years of experience to develop this ability.

Sometimes mass advertising is not needed to solve a problem. For example, in World War II our agency was asked to assist in helping to recruit young women in the Women Appointed for Volunteer Emergency Services (WAVES). We found a great number of inquiries were received from women interested in serving their country, but not many were signed up. We conducted a study that revealed that the WAVES recruiters had little or no understanding of the feelings of the girls they were interviewing. They were aloof and, without meaning to, literally scared many of the women out of joining.

We decided that the job for advertising in this situation was to reach, not the prospects, but rather the recruiters. A booklet was developed that actually was training material for the WAVES recruiters, and gave them a clear picture of their prospects.

Several months after this booklet was issued, Lieutenant H. A. Dudley, of the Navy Department's Bureau of Personnel, informed our agency that the handbook had done "a great deal within each office to increase enlistments."

Advertising doesn't always have to look like "advertising." Often the way the product is presented—the point of view—can be the determining factor in a successful campaign.

Some time ago our agency was called in to work with the Rev. William S. Bowdern, S.J., president of Campion High School in Prairie du Chien, Wisconsin, to help in solving an enrollment problem. Printed material he was sending to prospective students, we found, talked almost exclusively of the school facilities and faculty.

Our research found that in Catholic families the parents were the primary factor in the decision as to where the boy would attend school. To arouse interest of the parents as well as the boys, we shifted the focal point in the literature, making the boy the center of attention rather than the faculty members and school facilities. A message was directed to the parents in terms of benefit to the boy. On every page the line "your boy" was repeated. We also created a slogan which is still used: "Give Campion a boy and get back a man."

Father Bowdern later commented that "on every side I heard nothing but words of highest praise for the dignified advertising combined with real productive power."

In this somewhat sketchy illustration of how an advertising agency operates, I have tried to stress one basic fact: that advertising makes use of specialized selling skills in a manner and to an extent found in no other industry. Advertising executives work daily in difficult tasks that are, basically and almost solely, problem areas of communications. They have become quite capable in this field.

And I submit that the nation and our government have not been and are not now aware of the great use to which these skills could be put on behalf of our country.

I do not advocate that the *methods* used by advertising should be transferred, *in toto*, to the problems of international relations. Nor do I recommend that the government employ advertising agencies to do the job because, just as government leaders must make some changes in their propaganda policies to make use of advertising methods, so too, the advertising men who work for government must also change their methods to the degree necessary to fit in with the diplomatic policies of our government. I do say that the *techniques* of advertising, and the executives who are familiar with and understand these techniques, could be of immense value to our government. They should work under strict government supervision—but supervision by those who understand and appreciate the skills of advertising.

I must emphasize that not every advertising executive is a potential assistant and adviser to our government's propaganda program. There are other important requirements besides advertising competence. I believe the executive being considered for government service should have demonstrated that he is a humanist; he should have a background in community work; he should be thoroughly grounded in the liberal arts; and he should be acutely aware of our American heritage.

And of course, I would only recommend executives who adhere to the highest principles of advertising, and who feel strongly that the advertising community can help win the propaganda battle of the Cold War. I'd look for men like Charles Brower, head of Batten, Barton, Durstine & Osborn, who has been crusading to have the government recognize the great potential which admen can offer, and who once gave a speech with a 46-word title:

When in the hell is the United States of America going to stop acting like a rube at the fair—and start using the advertising and public relations skills with which it abounds to win the Cold War which it is presently losing like nobody's business?

> The Russians [he declared] really fear the day when America awakens to the fact that its great persuasive skills can be turned to the winning of minds. They know what our people are so slow to learn, that all their scientists, all their politicians and all their industry cannot create or duplicate the skills of American advertising. They can match our nuclear weapons and our rockets and our aircraft, but they cannot, this year or any other year, create the minds and machinery for massive communication that American advertising has built over the decades. . . .
>
> Advertising men must convince Congress and the White House that the time is ripe to use the great weapon. I believe that our industry must volunteer for active duty in this great war. . . . Advertising has the professional capacity to build great images, to stimulate interest, to modify public attitudes, to win loyalty, to close sales, to educate men and women about goods and services. Think what could happen if we in advertising and marketing and research and media trained our talents on the greatest products the world has ever known—democratic government, human freedom.

IX

Country Y

THE director of USIA's broadcasting operation, Henry Loomis, once appeared before a group to which I belong, the Foreign Relations Council of Chicago, to explain Voice of America. Mr. Loomis gave his audience many facts and figures on Voice. He was proud of the fact that it broadcast in 39 languages, and that it planned to double its Spanish-language broadcasting in Latin America; he was proud of the fact that VOA could count twenty million listeners; he was proud of the fact that with 87 transmitters the Voice was making a good fight against 2,500 transmitters manned by the Communists. He noted that in the opinion of Voice executives the British Broadcasting Company and Voice of America combined reached more listeners than did Moscow and Peiping. But when it came to defining the mission and goals of VOA, he faltered. Finally, he shrugged, tossed his hands upward and said: "It is a mission too complex to explain in the time I have. We provide the news and we try to tell the world what the United States is thinking and doing."

I think we should be proud of the fact that we broad-cast in so many languages; that we have an audience of twenty million souls who yearn for information. But I think it is disturbing that an official of the Voice of America should find the aims of his mission too complex to explain in an hour-long talk.

Is there a clear-cut objective? Is there a detailed plan for achieving this objective? If there is, there must be a way to explain to an intelligent group like the Foreign Relations Council of Chicago the means that are being taken to achieve that objective, so that they may judge if those means have a chance of accomplishing the desired results. Any good selling campaign can meet this require-ment. A campaign without a well-defined goal and the means to accomplish that goal is difficult to justify or explain.

In the months—indeed, years—that I have in an informal way propounded my belief that people trained in adver-tising should have a hand in formulating our nation's prop-aganda effort, I repeatedly have run into the obvious question: Well, what specifically would you do if *you* were running the show?

My answer is simple. I don't know.

I don't know specifically how I would attempt to sell Cadillac cars, trips to Japan, or any simple everyday prod-uct if the organization I administer were given one or all of those assignments. Nor do I know specifically how we will advertise the products we are now working with next year or the year after. Our current campaigns may lose their potency by then. Changing conditions may require a new copy approach, perhaps a change in media, or even changes in the packaging of the product. But we have the basic tools and the basic skills to study the markets for these products and eventually develop a campaign which would—hopefully—accomplish the objectives.

No more than a doctor can prescribe for a patient before he has examined him carefully, and often made required clinical tests, can the advertising man prescribe for a client before he carefully evaluates the specific problem. A good lawyer can build a case for a client, but not until he has all the facts. Doctors, lawyers and advertising specialists have the skills and tools required for their respective professions, but all need certain essential information to make these tools operate most effectively.

And so it would be with a government propaganda agency. The first task would be to conduct the specialized type of research required to build a selling campaign.

Nonetheless, we can here at least take a hypothetical situation to show how the techniques of advertising and selling can be applied to the job of international propaganda.

Let's assume now that our government has in Washington, and on call throughout the country, a large group of skilled advertising specialists whose job it is to aid the government in presenting our messages to the world.

It has been decided by our government that "Country Y" is now becoming important to the free nations of the world. Country Y is small, geographically removed from contact with many of our familiar institutions, and has recently become independent. It enjoys peace, but is a wary country; it does not know whether it should gravitate politically toward East or West, or remain neutral. It is strategically important to both the United States and Russia.

Our government, realizing that it is to its advantage to keep Country Y out of the Red orbit, calls in the assistance of the advertising specialists that have been recruited.

To these specialists, this is a job of selling our story and unselling the Communist story. The stakes are much higher than in a product campaign, but the objective is similar: Sell a good product to a market which doesn't know very much about the product, and through constructive selling offset the resistance that had been set up by a competitor.

As a first step, a planning group will meet. Immediately they call for a great deal of information which they have at hand, information gathered from the State Department, UN, USIA, CIA, the military, businessmen abroad, and any other available source.

This information, most of it statistical, must be available on every nation and region in the world. Present USIA methods for gathering and collating such information are not adequate to provide for the precise data needed for an effective propaganda operation. Much of the information is gathered informally; often it is simply opinion, or impressions stored in someone's memory, rather than the factual data that could be made available at a central point for objective analysis.

Much more emphasis must be given to the job of gathering good data on foreign countries, so that when the need for a specific campaign arises, time is not lost while the information is rounded up.

It is the kind of information any advertising agency

needs to know about the market before it can sell the client's product. It is immensely detailed, but the key items might include:

How is the population broken down—what percent is rural, what percent is urban?

How do the people earn their living? What do they receive as compensation? What will it buy?

What is the average age of the people? Is there a significant age group? Does this age group have any political importance?

What is the life expectancy? What are the principal health problems? What are the nutritional standards of the country? What is a typical diet? What are the physical characteristics of the people?

What are the housing standards of Country Y? Is privacy a factor in housing? Do families eat together or separately? How many meals a day do they eat? At what hours?

What are the educational levels, the educational institutions? How powerful are they?

How many ethnic and religious groups are there? What is their political and cultural significance?

What are the political parties? How large are they? How powerful are they? What are their platforms? Are they respected and believed?

What is the political history of Country Y? What are the principal political and social changes in the recent and not so recent past? What influences are these changes exerting?

Who are the present leaders, and who, if any, are

the deposed? What is their attitude toward other nations? Do they have recorded views on such matters as trade and tariffs, the United Nations, foreign aid, the Peace Corps, cultural exchanges?

What is the economic history of the country? What is its economic potential, based on raw materials and other factors? How can it best be helped if, indeed, it wants help?

What work is the Communist propaganda operation doing in the country?

With the answer to these key questions and many others, the planning group now has a paper picture of Country Y. They know a great deal, but they do not know enough. Experts in research are called upon to confirm all the information. But more importantly, they attempt to get a detailed picture of the emotional factors at work in the country.

Who are the thought leaders of Country Y, and how do they make their influence felt? Do they align themselves with the current political factions, or are they separate? What is their philosophy?

What does the word "freedom" mean to the people in Country Y? Can they define it? Can they define "democracy," "ideology," "totalitarianism," "capitalistic imperialism," "communism"—even the simple word "truth"?

What do the people of Country Y think of other peoples? How much do they know about other countries, and where did they get their information?

What do the people of Country Y dream about? What do they worry about? What do they do for enjoyment? What do they want for themselves and their children? What do they think about politicians; storekeepers; other races?

Much of this information can be gathered from educators, diplomatic officers and businessmen, but it must be verified by fieldwork, using all the latest psychological techniques to determine underlying motives that may not be apparent from what people say.

With an up-to-date statistical and emotional picture of Country Y in hand, our planning group is now ready to formulate a Copy Platform. This Copy Platform is the result of creative work. It will be designed to sell.

A way must be found to bring our basic products of peace and freedom to the people of Country Y in terms that can be easily identified and understood. Peace and freedom may have no meaning if explained in abstract terms. A way must be found to make them as real as the products which Country Y citizens use in their daily lives. This is the essence of any good selling program, and it takes a firm knowledge of the techniques of persuasion to discover dramatic ways to accomplish this end. People will not buy ideas that they cannot relate in some way to themselves.

Let's assume that agriculture is a prime industry in Country Y, and that it has a pest-control problem that is slowing its agricultural progress. If the rich yield of the land were not reduced by the insects, the people could grow enough of their staple crop to provide for themselves and establish export business as well.

Ideally, our government would supply pest-control facilities. With this action, our "client"—the U.S.A.—now takes on a practical value for the people of Country Y. And now our advertising experts mount the propaganda drive. In this case, the drive will be purely and simply an advertising campaign.

Our advertising will probably not look or sound much like the advertising we see in the U. S., because the task is different. Since advertising must play up our product benefit, our "ads" might be nothing more than easy-to-understand instructions on how to cooperate with whatever pest-control program is underway. (Or if our government decided not to supply help in controlling pests, the "ads" might give information on how the people can work on their own to control the insects.) These instructions would also carry the message that this help is being provided by the U. S.—perhaps a symbol of crossed flags of the two nations would adorn each instruction sheet.

Non-farm people in Country Y might be told, through paid advertising, how the U. S. is helping them to establish an export crop. These ads would explain in simple terms how sufficient *exports* mean they will be able to *import* many new goods, and how this in turn can bring about solid *economic* independence for the people of Country Y, which is the foundation of *political* independence. It should be made clear that the U. S. is not just a rich country giving away some surplus bug-killer in hopes of getting favorable trade agreements; rather, the U. S. is using this means to help Country Y help itself up the steep, rugged hill to a permanent place among the family of nations, and *away* from foreign domination.

The other side can be revealed, too; the persistent failure of Communist agriculture can be told and demonstrated in a hundred ways.

Whatever was done in this campaign, it would be done in the manner of advertising, with handbills, newspaper ads, radio announcements or whatever was needed to tell our story repeatedly and consistently. We would not depend on Country Y's government officials or news media to carry the ball.

Our media experts will, of course, determine how best to reach the people of Country Y with our messages:

> Are the newspapers well written? Are they believed? What segments of the population do they reach?
>
> Who prints the magazines? What are the characteristics of their readers?
>
> Will posters be effective? Are billboards allowed? Is humor, in the form of cartoons or special comic books, the best approach?
>
> Is radio a good medium? Are sets in wide distribution? What stations are listened to most? What time of day is best for broadcasting? If we broadcast in a native tongue are there regional differences in that tongue?

The media people may decide that the existing media in Country Y are insufficient to do the job, and they may recommend the establishment of a new medium. (Russia has done this in the Far East, distributing small battery-operated radio sets to the people. In keeping with the Communists' high regard for freedom of choice, the Russians added one twist. The sets were fixed so they could receive only one station—Radio Moscow.)

Once the media have been selected, the campaign to reach Country Y with our sales message begins. But the planning group does not rest there. Back go the specialists into the field to sample the effects of the campaign. If flaws are uncovered, the planning group meets to determine how to bolster the drive.

At the same time, our planning group must review continuing studies and evaluation of Communist efforts in Country Y.

(Incidentally, lest all the foregoing sound as though Country Y would be literally crawling with crew-cut young men with clipboards and pencils, making pests of themselves in search of opinions, I might point out that this type of research activity is carried out very extensively by thousands of advertisers here in the U. S. every day. Yet, statistically, very few Americans have ever been interviewed by a researcher. The quality of the research is vastly more important than the number of people researched.)

We must be prepared, in launching such a campaign, to meet opposition from our formidable competitor, who is experienced in the use of the techniques we would be using. He will no doubt have infiltrated Country Y with agitators and propaganda of all kinds. When Mr. Loomis of the Voice of America referred to the complexity of his mission, he meant the difficulties of broadcasting in almost twoscore foreign languages, of pitting 87 transmitters against 2,500 Russian and Chinese transmitters, of countering the Russian jamming techniques.

We must expect to find a flood of printed matter, and perhaps the channels over which we intend to broadcast will be effectively jammed. However, we must emphasize the content of our message and select the proper form for it before we determine the medium. It may be that radio broadcasts would be effective; and in that case we should use the Voice of America to persuade in the most telling manner, with popular programs with announcements to repeat our message over and over so that it will be heard and remembered.

Whatever the media we use, we must constantly bear in mind the strength and skill of our opponents. The Communists understand very well the complexities of selling. And selling is our task. There are two products on the market—one is the narrow ideology of Communism, the other the opportunity of free choice. Because there is no second chance for those who are beguiled by the false promises of the Communist pitchman, we must be sure that our sales message is presented with all the force at our command.

X

Plan for Action

THE United States is rich, powerful and genuinely humanitarian. Because of this we have a way of life that we believe to be the best in the world. We know how we have profited by democracy and our high standard of living.

But we have not been able to sell ourselves or our ideals to the world.

Yet the Russians, who offer to other nations the bleak prospect of totalitarian bondage, have relentlessly extended their power year by year until there is hardly a neutral nation in the world that is not in danger of coming under their influence.

Our ideal of fair play is unknown to them; honesty is a dream for children. Their strategists enjoy stealing U. S.-donated food from docks in India, stenciling it with *USSR*, and then shrugging off our protests. They exploit our most disinterested and humane efforts, as well as our vulnerable spots; they foster the image of the "ugly American" throughout the world.

Our response to the challenge is feeble and easily defeated. We do not stoop to the level of the Communists; we consider their offensive in the war of words "black propaganda."

But the means by which they spread it is not black magic. Long ago the Russians realized that advertising methods could be used for something besides selling goods. They are using simple psychological devices that all advertising men know. Through them they are able to make people who are not at all sympathetic to Communists do what the Russians want done; and the origin of the motivation is difficult to trace. We have at our disposal the same techniques, and we must use them. We do not have to stoop to the Communists' level of deceit and amorality; we can wage this war on the level of honesty and decency —and win. But we must be intelligently aware of how the enemy is using its threats of war and our desire for peace in order to subjugate the world.

If we are content to tell people that we have more automobiles, more radios, more refrigerators, toilets and bathtubs than any other nation, and that they should go and do likewise, we are guilty of the worst sin of any selling campaign—boasting about the product without offering its benefits.

And if we are content with giving aid without telling people why, and what our way of life is, then we are foolish. We have been so generous with the taxpayer's dollar that it is a miracle that our citizens pay taxes without rebelling; we have fed the hungry and clothed the poor. But in this war, generosity is not enough.

We must move to the attack in all parts of the world.

Our government has already made efforts in this direction, but, as I have suggested, these efforts are not enough. I believe that we should, first, adopt a realistic, unstoppable propaganda program that will reach every corner of the world with two badly needed messages—the truth about freedom and the truth about Communism; and, second, we must establish a government agency staffed with men who can research and carry out such a program.

How are we to do it? How can we get these skilled persuaders into the service of the government where they can be most effective?

First, of course, the country's Chief Executive must be convinced that such a move is wise, because it is up to him to appoint the key people. Then Congress must supply funds to implement an expanded program, and perhaps pass enabling legislation.

This in turn means that all who believe in the wisdom of such a program must make their feelings known in Washington. An idea of this sort is not apt to come into being on a wave of popular grass roots support. The average citizen may not become excited enough about our propaganda efforts to write a letter to his Congressman. But a small number of influential citizens—people who have won the respect of others—can turn the tide, because the people in Washington, by and large, are willing to give fair hearing to those in whom they have confidence.

I know that even if the policymaking group in Washington granted the wisdom of this idea, they might be reluctant to start any move toward enactment of such a program because it represents a tremendous change in concept.

But I think this change *must* be made. Many who have studied our propaganda efforts and declared them inadequate have suggested the establishment of an entirely new agency.

The specific proposals for such a government agency are many.

Former Senator William Benton has suggested a Department of International Public Affairs in the State Department to handle propaganda, technical information activities and cultural exchanges.

The Brookings Institution, after surveying U. S. foreign affairs, suggested in 1960 that a new Cabinet post be established—Secretary of Foreign Affairs, who would preside over the Secretary of State, Secretary of Foreign Economic Operations and Secretary of Information and Cultural Affairs.

In its special report on U. S. propaganda, *Printers' Ink* formulated recommendations which were a crystallization of the thinking of many others who are concerned with the problem of winning the War of Words.

Printers' Ink called for a Secretary of International Public Affairs in the State Department (co-equal with a Secretary of International Political Affairs and a Secretary of International Economic Affairs). The magazine also urged establishment of the Freedom Academy to train Cold War fighters; it suggests that our propaganda agency establish closer liaison with our businessmen overseas; and it asks for establishment of a Common Market of Ideas throughout the free world.

I propose the establishment of a completely new government Agency. This Agency, a Department of External

Relations, would be headed by an experienced advertising administrator who would have Cabinet rank. He would be directly responsible to the President, and would cooperate with all departments of government on matters involving propaganda and public relations.

Because our propaganda requirements embrace the entire world, and are of infinite variety, I propose that the Secretary for External Relations would require a large, full-time staff headquartered in Washington. His Agency would direct the efforts of specific departments charged with carrying our propaganda efforts aimed at specific countries. Each department would have liaison with a counterpart operation overseas. A special task-force unit would also be maintained to move quickly on unforeseen propaganda problems as they might arise.

The chart in this chapter gives some idea of the overall operation of such a new Agency. The Agency would be budgeted to make use of temporary personnel, recruited to help in special situations. These people might be drawn either from our own country, or from the nation posing the special problem.

On the chart, as an example, I have shown how this new Agency would operate in terms of Country Y. I have no preconceived notions as to the size and budget of the Department of External Relations. The permanent staff would be established in Washington, and would be enlarged as it proved its effectiveness and the need for its services increased.

It is probable that the new Agency would be called upon to help solve a number of problems dealing with our overseas image that may have no relationship to Com-

How a Department of External Relations Might Operate

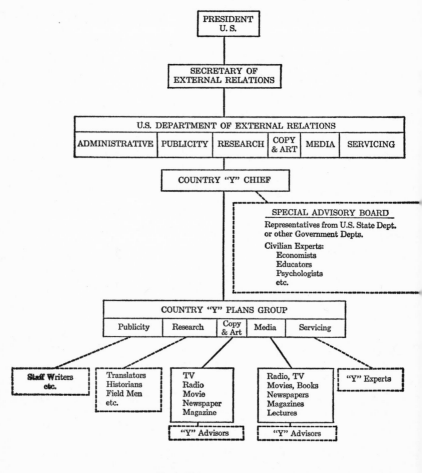

munism. Here is a specific example of that kind of problem: In late July, 1964, Secretary of State Dean Rusk, appearing before a Senate Judiciary subcommittee, urged enactment of a bill which he said would end the national-origins immigration quota system over a five-year period. One of his major arguments to the committee was, in his words, "The image held by many here and abroad of our immigration policy is one of discrimination." He went on to tell the subcommittee that of the 1½ million immigrants who entered the country from 1953 through 1962, only *34 percent* were quota immigrants. He added that this fact is not widely realized abroad and that unfriendly propaganda exploits still-remaining discriminations. Here is a job made to order for the Department of External Relations. Instead of changing our laws to combat the misconceptions, let's tell the true story of our immigration policy overseas.

The need for such clarifying campaigns is plain. There are numerous misconceptions which could be cleared up, including those about American crime, racial tensions, delinquency, and many others.

The cost of establishing a Department of External Relations would be substantial. But if it would decrease by even a small fraction the need for our current 46.7-billion-dollar defense budget, it would be money wisely spent. In fact, the operation of such an Agency might cost very little in the long run when considered as a basic investment in saving millions of human lives.

Whatever plan is most practical, it should be set in motion now. Our delay works in favor of the Communists, who have been working for a long time to plant destructive ideas in people's minds.

I do not propose that advertising men make foreign policy or attempt to influence the objectives of our President. An advertising executive does not manufacture what he sells. But once he has a product he believes in, he can present it in the best possible way to make people accept it. One important requirement of a good advertising man is that he knows not only his own product but that of his competitor. Counteroffensive is also needed. By acute observation, many a good advertising man would be able to discern the purposes and results of Communist propaganda, since he would be experienced in the uses of psychological devices. Once the Russian methods were recognized, he would know how they worked on the minds and wills of men; and he would know how to meet them with equally effective propaganda, to neutralize or destroy Communist gains.

Our government is aiming at the right target, but it has not yet learned how to hit it. I am not sure that we should blanket the world with a selling message for democracy; many of the countries which are now the Communists' prime targets are not ready for it. Nor do I advocate selling democracy like soap flakes. Any selling approach should be dictated by the market we are trying to reach.

When a farmer sows grain, he does not simply scatter it on top of the ground and hope it will take root. Instead, he prepares the soil carefully after testing it. He plants his seed deep in the furrows he has opened up. He covers and protects it. He returns constantly to fight off all the enemies which threaten the new seedlings. He nurses and nurtures his crop until the new growths have enough strength to stand alone.

We must do the same with the principles we hold so precious. They will not take root if they are simply scattered.

The Communists have a long start on us; they have sown the world with poisonous weeds. It is time now for us to take a long look into the future, for it will be a long struggle. We must make a careful study of long-range objectives, plan our strategy, and understand our weapons. We can still overcome the untruths the Russians have planted. We can eradicate the image of the "ugly American" and replace it with a true image of what America is.

AFTERWORD

This work covers the essential substance of one of the principal interests of the study now being conducted by the House Subcommittee on International Organizations and Movements, of which I am Chairman. I concur wholeheartedly that we have had far too much emphasis on the military and economic aspects of international politics. I am also convinced that the determination of the struggle, or, to restate the proposition, the achievement of our objectives, will be determined by our success in the non-military, non-economic areas, or in the ideological field. Therefore, alerting the American public to THE STRATEGY OF PERSUASION with an affirmative plan of action is timely and essential.

This book makes a strong case for salesmanship in international politics, and I generally agree with its findings and conclusions and applaud its recommendations. Government, and Americans, and for that matter the free world, must be made aware of the true nature of the struggle. That is why this book is important. It is a significant contribution for Americans in and out of Government to understand the true nature of our international struggle.

—REP. DANTE B. FASCELL (D)
4th District, Florida
Member, House Committee on
Foreign Affairs
Chairman, Subcommittee on
International Organizations
and Movements

Bibliography

I. Books:

1. Barghoorn, Frederick C., *The Soviet Cultural Offensive,* Princeton University Press, Princeton, 1960.
2. Britt, Steuart Henderson, *The Spenders,* McGraw-Hill, New York, 1960.
3. Cantril, Hadley, *Soviet Leaders and Mastery Over Man,* Rutgers University Press, New Jersey, 1960.
4. Carroll, Wallace, *Persuade or Perish,* Houghton Mifflin, Boston, 1948.
5. Creel, George, *How We Advertised America,* Harper & Bros., New York, 1920.
6. De Koster, Lester, *Vocabulary of Communism,* Wm. B. Eerdmans Publishing Co., Grand Rapids, Michigan, 1963.
7. Douglas, William O., *Strange Lands and Friendly People,* Harper, 1951.
8. Hansen, Prof. Alvin, *Economic Issues of the 1960's,* McGraw-Hill, 1960.
9. Hoover, J. Edgar, *A Study of Communism,* Holt, Rinehart and Winston, 1962.
10. Irwin, Will, *Propaganda and the News,* McGraw-Hill, 1936.
11. Kennedy, Robert, *Just Friends and Brave Enemies,* Harper and Row, New York, 1962.

12. Lerner, Max, *Ideas Are Weapons,* The Viking Press, New York, 1939.

13. Liebling, A. J., *The Press,* Ballantine, New York, 1961.

14. Mayo, H. B., *Introduction to Democratic Theory,* Oxford University Press, New York, 1960.

15. Mock, J. R. and Cedric Larson, *Words That Won the War,* Princeton University Press, Princeton, New Jersey, 1939.

16. Morgan, Clifford T., *Introduction to Psychology,* McGraw-Hill, New York, 1961.

17. Munson, Gorham, *Twelve Decisive Battles of the Mind,* Greystone Press, New York, 1942.

18. Nixon, Richard M., *Six Crises,* Doubleday, 1962.

19. Overstreet, Harry and Bonaro, *The War Called Peace,* Norton, New York, 1961.

20. Overstreet, Harry and Bonaro, *What We Must Know About Communism,* W. W. Norton, New York, 1958.

21. Peroutka, Ferdinand, *Democratic Manifesto,* Voyages Press, New York, 1959.

22. Peroutka, Ferdinand, reference to Robert C. Tucker, *Stalin and The Uses of Psychology,* (p. 473).

23. Peroutka, Ferdinand, introduction by Adolf A. Berle.

24. Peterson, H. C., *Propaganda for War,* University of Oklahoma Press, 1939.

25. Ponsonby, Arthur, *Falsehood in Wartime,* Dutton, New York, 1929.

26. Potter, David, *People of Plenty,* University of Chicago Press, Chicago, Illinois, 1954.

27. Reeves, Rosser, *Reality in Advertising,* Knopf, New York, 1961.

28. Schlesinger, Arthur M., *Prelude to Independence,* Knopf, New York, 1958.

29. Schwartz, Dr. Fred, *You Can Trust the Communists* (*To Be Communists*), Prentice-Hall, 1960.

30. Stephens, Oren, *Facts To a Candid World,* Stanford University Press, Stanford, California, 1955.

31. Strausz-Hupé & associates, *Protracted Conflict,* Harper & Row, 1963.

32. Viereck, George Sylvester, *Spreading Germs of Hate,* H. Liveright, New York, 1930.

II. Periodicals:

1. *Advertising Age,* Alex I. Osborn in February 13, 1961 issue.

2. *Advertising Age,* Henry Mayers article in March 20, 1961 issue, Vol. 32, No. 12, pp. 83-90.

3. *Advertising Age,* Excerpts from Charles Brower's speech in April 9, 1962 issue.

4. *Advertising Age,* Burton Hotveldt article in June 5, 1961 issue.

5. *ADA World,* Hubert H. Humphrey, "Make Change Our Ally, Not Our Enemy," May, 1961.

6. *Baltimore Sun,* "Getting America's Story Across," August 13, 1961.

7. *Chicago Daily News,* Sydney J. Harris, "Nations Can Be Betrayed By Slogans," August 1, 1961.

8. *Chicago Sun Times,* column by Richard Elden (p. 4), August 28, 1961.

9. *Houston Post,* Felton West, "Voice of America," February 25, 1962.

10. *Intelligence Digest,* edited by Kenneth de Courcy, August, 1961, No. 273, p. 2.

11. *Madison Avenue,* Allen Schwartz in September, 1960 issue.

12. *Marketing,* Dave Levy article, January 27, 1961.

13. *New York Times,* Tom Whitney in September 30, 1956 edition.

14. *New York Times,* Max Frankel in October 8, 1958 edition.

15. *New York Times,* Dr. Ernest Dichter (president of the Institute of Motivational Research, Croton-on-Hudson, N.Y.) in October 17, 1958 edition.

16. *Newsweek,* "Is Truth the Best Weapon?" September 18, 1961.

17. *Printers' Ink,* "Communications Crisis: The War We're Losing," September 14, 1962.

18. *The Reporter,* Edmond Taylor, "Political Warfare," September 14, 1961.

19. *Soviet Geography: Review and Translation,* December 1960, Vol. I, No. 10.

20. *Soviet Geography:* January, 1961, Vol. II, No. 1.

21. *Soviet Geography:* March, 1961, Vol. II, No. 3.

22. *Time,* October 12, 1962.

23. *U. S. News and World Report,* August 15, 1960.

24. *U. S. News and World Report,* July 1, 1963.

25. *Wall Street Journal,* August 15, 1963.

III. Other Material (*Reports, speeches, pamphlets, correspondence, etc.*)

1. Brorby, Melvin, "We Ask Ourselves Four Questions," based on talks delivered in Atlanta, Dallas, Denver and Chicago, February-March, 1958, copyright 1958, AAAA.

2. Burnett, Leo, "What Is This Thing Called Advertising?" speech to the Los Angeles Advertising Club, February 7, 1961.

3. Burnett, Leo, reference in above speech to Walter Teplin's book, *Advertising—A New Approach,* Hutchinson, London, 1960.

4. Coste, Felix W., *"The Troubled Americans,"* an address before the Atlantic Advertising Club, Copyright 1961, by Outdoor Advertising, Inc.

5. Espenshade, Edward B., Jr., Department of Geography, Northwestern University, Evanston, Illinois, letter to Arthur Meyerhoff, June 20, 1961.

6. Freedoms Foundation, 1961 Announcement of the 13th Annual National and School Awards Program, "The American Way of Life."

7. Harding, Harry, "Purpose: Growth," speech presented at the 1961 American Association of Advertising Agencies, Annual Meeting, April 22, 1961, White Sulphur Springs, Virginia.

8. Hearings before the Subcommittee on International Organizations and Movements of the Committee on Foreign Affairs, House of Representatives, Parts I and II, March-May, 1963.

9. Lasswell, Harold A., "Propaganda," Encyclopedia Britannica, 1960, Vol. 18.

10. Loomis, Henry, "The Voice of America Will Be 20 Years Old Next Week," address before the National Press Club, February 21, 1962.

11. Marstellar, William A., "The Significance of Advertising," an address before the 40th Annual Convention, Illinois State High School Press Association, University of Illinois, Urbana, Illinois, September 16, 1960.

12. "Meet the Press," NBC, August 4, 1963, W. Averell Harriman as guest.

13. "Meet the Press," NBC, April 5, 1964, Dr. Milton Eisenhower as guest.

14. Mikoyan, Anastas, talk to managers of trade organizations, directors of large state stores and shop assistants, October 17, 1955.

15. Mortimer, Charles O., "Consumer Persuasion—Black Art or Key to Economic Progress?" address by chairman of General Foods Corporation in accepting Annual Applause Award from the Sales Executives Club of New York, September 13, 1960.

16. Murrow, Edward R., former head of the United States Information Agency, statements and speeches:
"Who Speaks for America?" address before the National Press Club, Washington, D.C., May 24, 1961.
"The Divided World," address before Johns Hopkins Hospital, Baltimore, Maryland, June 13, 1961.
"Improved Communications for Better Understanding," address before the Poor Richard Club, Philadelphia, Pennsylvania, September 14, 1961.
Statement before the Subcommittee on Departments of State, Justice and Commerce, the Judiciary, and Related Agencies, Senate Committee on Appropriations, September 19, 1962.
"America's Intellectual Image Abroad," address before the American Council on Education.

17. Reports on Hearings before a Subcommittee of the Committee on Appropriations, House of Representatives, 87th Congress, 1962.

18. Reports on Hearings before a Subcommittee of the Committee on Appropriations, Senate, 87th Congress, 1962.

19. Reports (Semiannual) of the United States Advisory Commission on Information:
To the Congress of the United States, the 12th.
Report of the U. S. Advisory Commission on Information, January, 1957.
Same, 13th Report, January, 1958.

Same, 14th Report, March, 1959.

Same, 15th Report, March, 1960.

Same, 16th Report, January, 1961.

Same, 17th Report, February, 1962.

20. Repplier, Ted, "A Proposal About America's Propaganda," address to the Board of Directors of the Advertising Council, March, 1961.

21. Repplier, Ted, "We, the People, and the Idea War, from *Papers from the 1957 Annual Meeting,* copyright 1957, AAAA, New York.

22. Terkel, Studs, radio program, "The Wax Museum," WFMT, Chicago, Illinois, interview with two Russians accompanying the Exhibit of Soviet Technical Books, June 24, 1963.

23. Townsend, W. S., "The Townsend Method of Mass Persuasion—The Townsend Method of Advertising Evaluation," loaned to Arthur Meyerhoff Associates, January, 1944.

24. United States Information Agency material:
Communist Propaganda Activities in The Middle East, Aegean Area, 1960.
Communist Propaganda Activities in the Arab States and Israel, January, 1960-June, 1961.
Communist Propaganda Activities in Latin America, 1960.
Communist Propaganda Activities in South Asia, 1961.
Communist Propaganda Activities in Africa, January, 1960-May, 1961.
Communist Propaganda Activities in The Far East, 1961.
Chinese Communist Policy and Propaganda, 1960.

25. Developments in Communist Bloc International Broadcasting in the First Half of 1962.

26. Overseas Television Developments in 1961.

27. The Entire World Watched.

28. USIA and the Alliance for Progress.

USIA News Releases:

29. Attorney General Discusses Meredith Case on VOA, No. 51.

30. Full Coverage of Cuban Crisis Reported World-Wide by USIA, No. 53.

31. Reds' Secret Radio Stations Tripled Output, USIA Reveals, No. 45.

32. Reprint from Machinists' Weekly Newspaper (on Everett Dee Fairchild, "Little Moe" cartoonist.)

33. USIA Reports to Congress:
    15th Report to Congress, July 1-December 31, 1960.
    16th Report to Congress, January 1-June 30, 1961.
    17th Report to Congress, July 1-December 31, 1961.
    18th Report to Congress, January 1-June 30, 1962.

34. World Reaction to Soviet Resumption of Testing, August 17, 1962.

35. Presenting America Abroad Through Television.

36. The Agency in Brief, January, 1962.

37. The Overseas Film Program.

38. Portraying American Culture to the World.

39. Telling America's Story Abroad Through Press and Publications.

40. Zellerbach, J. D., "Alliance and Responsibility," in "A Confidential Analysis of Economic Developments," *Committee for Economic Development*, February, 1961. Vol. VI, No. I.

ARTHUR E. MEYERHOFF

ARTHUR E. MEYERHOFF, who was born in 1895 in Chicago, is one of America's outstanding advertising men. His career in sales began when he was in grammar school and sold the Chicago *Evening American* Newspapers—then 2¢—at the entrance to the stock yards on the South Side. By 1929, after service with the A.E.F. in World War I, he had his own advertising agency, Neisser & Meyerhoff, which started with billings of $100,000. Since 1941 the author has been president of Arthur Meyerhoff Associates, Inc., with billings of $15,000,000 annually. "I have spent my entire life selling commercial products," writes the author. "However, I have long had what amounts to a second occupation—applying the techniques of selling and advertising to public service groups and causes. I have always believed that the same techniques and know-how that can move the products of American industry can also move the American people in support of worthwhile causes."